D0874027

The Little Book
of Dog Care

The Little Book of Dog Care

EXPERT ADVICE ON GIVING
YOUR DOG THEIR BEST LIFE

ACE TILTON RATCLIFF

SIMON ELEMENT

NEW YORK LONDON TORONTO SYDNEY NEW DELHI

SIMON
ELEMENT

An Imprint of Simon & Schuster, Inc.
1230 Avenue of the Americas
New York, NY 10020

First Simon Element hardcover edition July 2023

SIMON ELEMENT is a trademark of Simon & Schuster, Inc.

For information about special discounts for bulk purchases,
please contact Simon & Schuster Special Sales at 1-866-506-1949
or business@simonandschuster.com.

The Simon & Schuster Speakers Bureau can bring authors to your
live event. For more information or to book an event, contact the
Simon & Schuster Speakers Bureau at 1-866-248-3049 or visit
our website at www.simonspeakers.com.

Interior design by Laura Levatino
Illustrations by Twins Design Studio

Manufactured in the United States of America

10 9 8 7 6 5 4 3 2 1

Library of Congress Cataloging-in-Publication Data
has been applied for.

ISBN 978-1-9821-7303-6
ISBN 978-1-9821-7305-0 (ebook)

FOR ROLAND, MY HEART DOG

AND RUPERT, MY HEART DEMON

Contents

Introduction

There is a dog sitting behind me on my chair[1] as I write right now. He's been behind me for every word of this book so far; he sits there whenever I write. He's not very big—he weighs about ten pounds soaking wet, and most of that weight is in his ears—but somehow, he always manages to take up more of the chair than I do.

His name is Rupert. I can feel him breathing against my spine; occasionally he lets out a contented *huff* to let me know I'm doing a good job of keeping him warm, though he'd really prefer if we'd go cuddle on the bed now, pretty please. I tend to write late at night, tapping away at the keyboard until the early hours of the morning. Rupert wants to crawl beneath blankets and nestle between pillows starting at 9:00 pm on the dot, but he compromises by keeping me company instead. Rupert came into my life as a teeny-tiny Rat-Terrier-mix puppy just a few weeks after my heart dog,[2] Roland, died unexpectedly in early 2021, right before the pandemic began. Rupert isn't my only dog, though the whole pack would probably tell you I spoil him the most (especially since he's the youngest).

---

1 Really, our chair. Or maybe his chair that I'm just borrowing.

2 There are dogs and then there are heart dogs. Heart dogs occupy a
   special place in your heart and are comparable to soul mates. Canine
   companions forever, if you will. Like Roland, Rupert is a heart dog—but he
   is also a terror, which makes him my demon dog. Your mileage may vary.

If they were given the option, all my dogs would somehow manage to sit in my lap while I write—or really, while I do anything sedentary at all. Bashi, the probably five-year-old Papillon mix who is slightly bigger than the rest, curls his blond body into the smallest ball possible on the dog bed that lives permanently under my desk, tucking his nose beneath his feathered tail. Beside him, Ezra stretches out more languidly. He's a shadow in Terrier form except for the smattering of white dots over his right eyebrow. We think he's about eight, but that number could be off since he's only got seven teeth left in his head. Old man Henry, the last dog in the pack—incontinent, wearing a diaper, either pacing incessantly or snoring so loudly I can hear him all the way from the living room through the mostly closed office door—is somewhere between thirteen and eternal. He's the only one more fond of food than my company, but I don't take that personally at his age—I'd feel the same.

All four of them are rescues. The bright flash of Bashi across the Oakland road in front of us had my husband and me slamming on the brakes and throwing open the car doors on the way home from date night, cornering and ushering Bashi into my waiting arms so he wasn't hit by a car. Rupert was found wandering the streets of Miami with his mom right after we moved cross-country back to my hometown in South Florida, my heart newly broken by the death of Roland and terrified by the way the world was changing. Ezra was the smallest, grouchiest rescue left at my local animal shelter in December, the year Roland died; I thought he might bite me when I tried to say hello, but he was too scared to even move. Now I can't get him off of me. As for Henry, well, I met Henry while dropping off donations at another local shelter. (I couldn't leave without taking a look around, even though I knew it would break my heart to not be able to bring everyone home.) I came back after a long weekend of thinking about him. Almost everybody comes to the shelter looking for a puppy. Nobody wants the rickety bag of bones who looks like he's already lived a rough life. He was the only dog left after everybody else had been adopted. I couldn't just leave him. I couldn't leave any of the dogs in my pack behind.

I am, one might say, a sucker for animals in general, dogs clearly included. Rescues are my particular forte; my household menagerie currently contains three jumping spiders, seven ball pythons,[3] three cats,[4] the aforementioned four dogs,[5] and more isopods than I can count.[6] After a few years of thinking I might become a veterinarian (even sitting in on a spay surgery!), I married one instead.[7] My veterinarian-husband, Dr. Derek Calhoon, spends most of his time working emergency locally here in South Florida, though we also co-own a veterinary practice called Harper's Promise (HP). HP is focused on in-home visits for hospice, palliative care, and euthanasia. We've been running since 2017, back when our dog Harper (who started out as my dog, before Derek fell in love with her) got sick with congestive heart failure. Derek has read this book front to back through all sundry drafts, which makes it veterinarian approved. Besides proofreading and fact-checking, he also helps make a dent in our prodigious vet

---

3   Three of whom are rescues.

4   All three were saved from euthanasia after cars or other unknown objects pulverized various combinations of their pelvises and legs/hips.

5   Rescue dogs forever! Henry, Dog bless him, died in November 2022, .

6   Really, they just keep multiplying!

7   Way easier than all the schooling, though somehow I still ended up in a household paying back student loans.

bills . . . but doesn't exactly stop from adding to the menagerie when he texts pictures from the office of broken babies who desperately need help and a loving home.

Although I'd spent my whole life with dogs, Harper's illness was the first time as an adult that I was in the position of making decisions about a dog's death. At the time, I was on the tail end of six years working as a mortician, licensed in the state of California as a funeral director, embalmer, and crematory operator. I'd spent plenty of time with death. I knew I didn't want Harper dying in an austere medical setting, paws scrabbling against a stainless-steel exam table and the smell of other dogs' fear the last thing she remembered. So instead, we euthanized her at home after a too-short day hiking at the park, eating hamburgers and a Puppuccino after we finished. Then we went to the pet store and let her pick out a toy before adding Derek's name to the last tag she would ever wear on her collar.

When I gently lowered her body into her casket and tucked a blanket around her that was the same turquoise color as her collar, her long white fur was still soft from the kitchen-sink bath I'd given her the day before. I surrounded her with roses and alstroemeria and tucked a treat shaped like a bone beneath her paw before we drove to the crematory, where I placed her body inside the retort and, an hour later, gently swept out her bones to bring her home in an urn. Throughout Harper's death and dying, I was able to make the best decisions I could for both of us, and I've since had the privilege and honor of guiding hundreds of other pets from life through the same processes of death and dying. Each and every one is special in their own way, from their scales to their whiskers to their claws to their hooves, but there's something distinctive about dogs that makes them incomparable. Of course, many of those dogs I've helped die have been my own.

My mom frequently muses that "life is a series of dogs," and my life has certainly always been that way. While my mom was pregnant, there were two Golden Retrievers watching over me. I can't remember Justin and Goldie very well, but I definitely recognize them in pictures. One of my very first memories is digging in the dirt at my Mama Jo's, feeling curled white fur beneath my palm while petting her dogs, Cuddles and Twinkie. (I also remember that stink of their dog breath—and, I admit, to kinda liking that particular grossness.) I was a military brat with a fighter pilot dad, and my family moved to England when I was a toddler. Our first Christmas there, my parents took me to pick out a puppy from a litter of Cavalier King Charles Spaniels. In the cloudless night sky, the stars twinkled bright as the lights on our tree—which, of course, seemed like the perfect name for my new pup. My parents both swear that their new English neighbors must have thought the Americans who had moved in were absolutely out of their minds, standing in the backyard and yelling, "Tree! Tree!" at all hours to get the dog to come back inside.

We eventually moved back to the States and settled in Florida, where mom brought home a tiny Weimaraner puppy named Sophie. That dog was a bundle of berserk energy who desperately needed a daily five-mile run to maintain sanity. Another Weim joined the pack when mom decided Sophie needed a friend. When we got to the house that had advertised puppies for sale, they were all gone. We went home with the neglected momma dog, Jade, instead.

Growing up in a house that always had dogs, I have found it nearly impossible to function without one as an adult. On my first solo trip as a tween to visit my paternal grandparents in Colorado, they borrowed a big dog from a neighbor so I could actually get some rest in their guest bedroom. Without a dog's steady breathing to lull me to sleep, I simply lay there in the dark, staring at the ceiling. Once I finally left for college, I didn't last a single semester without a dog. I had been eyeing want ads before my professors even started talking about final exams. Admittedly, the purchase of Roland was rather ill-advised, given that I was a nineteen-year-old living in student housing (where dogs weren't allowed), but I'd spent the last few months absolutely miserable without one. I drove out to the middle of nowhere, Central Florida, "just to look" at the Chihuahua puppies, and I was absolutely smitten with the lot of them. After the runt of the litter sat down beside me and carefully placed his tiny paw on my thigh before looking up at me with his strangely human eyes, I simply had to bring him home with me. The universe clearly commanded it, housing rules be damned.

After Roland came Harper,[8] then Bashi, and on and on and on till the present day. My home altar has far more pet memorializations on it now than it did when I was a teenager—in part because Derek and I tend to bring home the dogs with the worst health problems, given our unique capacity to make the end of their lives not just manageable but full of love, joy, and kindness—and I know that the rest of my life will mean loving more of them and having all of them eventually break my heart. I truly believe that the furry (usually) four-legged[9] creatures we've been lucky enough to invite into our homes[10] are saints. In my opinion, sainthood requires one to become

---

8   *Obviously*, Roland needed a playmate. Would you expect anything else from me at this point?

9   But sometimes fewer!

10 For a period of time that is *never* long enough.

the embodiment of love, and I dare you to find me a better description for dogs.

Dogs love you. They don't just *love* you; they downright adore you. They desperately want to be around you, even if all you're doing is staring at a tiny, bright screen and bashing away on a keyboard to line up words in sentences that mean nothing to them. You walk through the front door and your mere presence is proof that the universe is in order once more, because it all went to hell the second you left. Is this dog perhaps not your dog, but a dog you've never met before? That's fine. You're best friends now! Every meal is the best goddamn meal they've ever had. Crumbs on the floor? Divine cuisine. Every pee is a bathroom break made of magic. Dogs bring their entire selves to each and every experience, and usually that self is one made of bliss at the absolute delight of existence. Every dog I've ever met has been like this.

(Of course, this outlook tends to focus on a happy dog versus an unhappy one, but trust that I've met enough dogs at this point to know plenty of them bring anxiety, stress, fear, and sometimes what feels like anger to living, too. I'll be damned if they don't bring those feelings 110 percent, though. Problematic dogs happen, yes, but usually it's our fault, not theirs.)

Although dogs might have us beat in embracing the divine ideals of love and joy, they're also not that much different from us humans in many ways. They feel emotions the same way we do, from love to fear to anger.[11] They need care the way we do, like well-balanced meals and regular exercise. They have

---

11   Yes, seriously: Simon Worrall, *National Geographic*, September 8, 2017, "Dogs Have Feelings—Here's How We Know," https://www .nationalgeographic.com/animals/article/dog-brain-feelings-mri -gregory-berns.

to see doctors for regular checkups like we do—and sometimes they even need to make a visit to the ER. The commonalities we have with canines are part of why they slot so easily into our lives and our hearts.

If you're reading this book, either you've got a dog, you've had dogs, you're planning to get a dog, or you have friends who are talking about bringing a dog into their lives. Maybe you want to know the basics of loving and caring for your pooch. Maybe you want to level up to meet the needs of your pet in a way you didn't know how to before or simply couldn't when you were younger. Maybe you're thinking about a dog but want to know exactly what you're getting into before you commit. Maybe you love dogs and you want to learn more about them. Whatever the reason, friend, I'm very excited to be along for this dog journey with you. I've learned so much about dogs through my lifetime with them and I'm lucky enough to learn more about them with every dog I meet, whether because I've brought them home as a new puppy or because I'm stroking their ears as their family says a final goodbye. Every day, I learn how to be a better owner for my dogs. I also learn a little more from them about how to be more present in each moment, more excited about the mundane experiences that make up my day-to-day, and more willing to live my life through their guiding principle of unmitigated joy. I hope that after reading this book, you're able to do the same.

CHAPTER 1

Finding Your Dog

The most important step in this book—the singularly focused, inherently crucial, can't-do-the-rest-until-you've-managed-this absolute necessity—is procuring a dog. This is actually a lot easier than you might expect it to be. Well, let me rephrase: this *can* be a lot easier than you expect it to be. Being married to a veterinarian certainly means I have a direct source,[12] but you don't have to become a part stakeholder in your partner's copious scholastic debt in order to acquire a dog. That's just a bonus.

I'll run you through the how and where (and how much) of acquiring a dog in this chapter. There are pros and cons for each approach. Generally speaking, my household now only acquires dogs as rescues. I am of the opinion that the world is full of dogs who desperately need homes. Purchasing a dog via a breeder can be both an ethical dilemma and the root of medical complications. However, I fully expect that you'll want to do research beyond this cute little book—you need to figure out all the details about the dog who's going to be right for you, even beyond how dang adorable they are.

Let's get to it.

---

12 A dealer, as it were?

Choosing the Dog Who's Right for You

All right, friend, let's talk about the things you need to think about when selecting the dog who's right for you. One of the biggest topics to rise to the top of the list is the size of your dog. In our house, we have a strict limit of fifteen pounds or under. Do I absolutely adore giant Pit Bulls with heads the size of small cars and bodies that can destroy living rooms in a single tail wag? Yes, more than anything. I am fortunate that I live in a three-bedroom house with a fairly large, fenced backyard, which is great for big dogs. But I also have a degenerative disease that makes my joints easily dislocate and I weigh ninety-five pounds on a good day, so managing a dog who can drag me down the street if they get too excited is something I have to think about when adopting. Size and weight are necessary considerations about the dog who's going to be right for you.

One of the big issues with the hunt for the perfect dog (especially if you're looking for a smaller pup) is running into the term "teacup." As someone who adores Chihuahuas, I can't tell you how many times I've read the phrase "teacup Chihuahua for sale!" Synonyms include "pocket-size," "toy," "tiny toy," or "miniature." Often breeders use these terms to market the smallest dog in the litter as something special or particularly valuable. There's no such thing as a teacup Chihuahua, though, y'all. I'm sorry to burst your bubble, but it's a marketing ploy.

Next up on the list is energy. Of course, dogs are going to need *some* kind of exercise on a daily basis, even if it's just a quick jaunt outside to potty. Most dogs need more than that, whether that be playtime, brain stimulation, or straight exercise.[13] Almost all of my pack of fifteen-pounds-and-under do

---

13   Preferably all three, to be completely honest.

two miles of fast-paced walking daily, and if they had their druthers we'd do it twice a day.[14] Henry is the singular exception; due to his age, he has fairly gnarly arthritis in his spine—but you best believe he gets taken in a doggy stroller so he, too, can enjoy the mental stimulation of being outside the house. What kind of dog is going to fit into the lifestyle you're currently living? Do you have time to walk a high-energy breed multiple times a day? Or are you looking for someone who spends more time in couch potato mode? Are you willing to commit to hours of intense training regularly, or is mastering sit, stay, and shake enough?

Figuring out the specifics of your life is important in these considerations, too. Do you have kids? Obviously, you need a dog who gets along with littles. Do you have cats or other pets in your house? You need a dog who isn't going to try to chase and/or eat other family members. Do you have a backyard your dog can use to toilet, or do you have to walk down a set of stairs every time they have to pee?[15] Like with the rest of life, you can't control for all variables, but making sure they're forefront in the decision-making process will make your life easier down the line.

Energy levels tend to bleed into age, too. Many people who read this book are probably intent upon acquiring a puppy, but you don't have to start with a young dog. There are plenty of geriatric dogs out there who need homes, trust me. A puppy or younger dog is (usually) going to have more energy. Middle-aged and old dogs (usually) have slowed down a bit, which tends toward a different lifestyle and commitment. Geriatric dogs may also have a host of other health issues, depending on the breed.

---

14 My knees disagree.

15 Especially when you're potty training!

Also, you're typically going to have more time with a puppy than you do with a geriatric dog, simply because the world is cruel and dogs don't live long enough.

The breed of your desired dog is going to play a part in many of the characteristics described. (See: my sadness at not being able to provide the right home to a massive pit bull.) Obviously, a Chihuahua (or Chihuahua mix) is going to fit my necessary characteristics better than a Golden Retriever. Again, I have an ethical and medical preference for rescues and mixed-breed dogs, so I tend toward Chihuahua and Terrier mixes instead of purebred pups. Breed characteristics will also help with preferences for characteristics like coat. I've owned long-haired dogs, and I find that it's a lot of work, both the shedding and the grooming. In the future, it'll take a lot to tempt me into adopting a long-haired dog over one with short fur.[16]

It's important to note here that many people start their search hunting for hypoallergenic dogs, or dogs who have little likelihood of causing an allergic reaction in someone who is allergic to dogs. Somewhere along the road, "hypoallergenic" became synonymous with "doesn't shed." There are types of dogs that shed less fur than others, but research has found that some of the breeds advertised as hypoallergenic have some of the highest levels of the primary dog allergen.[17] While there are dogs who shed less than others (a hairless breed may be the right call for you, versus a Husky),

---

16 I said the same thing about owning another white dog after Harper died because you could see her long fur on *everything* but went ahead and adopted Rupert immediately, so I cannot necessarily be trusted.

17 Gemma Johnstone, "Does a Completely Hypoallergenic Dog Exist?," American Kennel Club, July 20, 2021, https://www.akc.org/expert -advice/dog-breeds/do-hypoallergenic-dog-exist.

there is no guarantee that these breeds mean you won't have an allergic reaction. Allergies can sometimes be managed via good housekeeping, having hardwood floors instead of carpeted, and even immunotherapy shots administered by a doctor, but some people are allergic to dog spit as well as dog dander (their skin cells). It's more about your immune system than the dog. Every dog sheds. Every dog produces dander. If, during your search for the perfect dog, you run into the word "hypoallergenic," whoever is using it wants to dupe you with false advertising.[18]

The last thing you're going to need to consider when bringing a dog into your life is the cost of actually adopting them, but I'll talk about that in the next section as I discuss options for where you adopt your dog from.

You may find that you have other expectations for the dog who's coming into your life. That's fine, baby. This is your dog. You're going to be living with them for up to fifteen or more years. Do the work of making the right decisions *before* you're already committed. You and your dog will appreciate it.

Where to Find Your Dog

Typically speaking, there are a few major ways to go about bringing a dog into your life: through a shelter or adoption agency or via a breeder or storefront. You may not find the perfect place right away, but that's okay. Be patient. The wait for the right pup can be tough, but it will pay off. I promise! Where a dog comes from is important. Your commitment in time, energy, effort, and love is more important.

---

18   And if it's a hypoallergenic teacup dog, you best run outta there.

Shelter Adoption

As I've said a million times before, our house strictly adopts rescues. Overpopulation is a huge issue around the world, and there are more dogs than ever who desperately need someone to spoil them rotten for the rest of their lives. There's something about a rescued dog (of any age!)—the gratitude and joy at having a home, regular meals, and love is truly present in every interaction you have with them.

If you've decided that adopting from a shelter is the best call for your family, I encourage you to seek local shelter adoption first. This gives you the opportunity to make a difference directly in your community. It also means that you can visit in person, to meet your dog and interact with them one-on-one. A quick Google search should bring up shelters that are near you. You may hear about your local ASPCA (American Society for the Prevention of Cruelty to Animals, which was established in 1866)[19] or the Humane Society.[20] There may be a shelter with a different name or association near you that makes a huge impact, like local animal control. Do some research and be ready to visit more than one place in the great search for the right dog. Maybe even check out Pets and People Together[21], a collaborative effort between leading animal welfare groups focused on ensuring potential adopters turn to shelters first when trying to find a pet.

Shelter pets often get a bad rap for having behavioral issues, but most of the animals who come to shelters end up there through no fault of their own. Moving and landlord

---

19   ASPCA, https://www.aspca.org/.

20   The Humane Society of the United States, https://www
      .humanesociety.org/.

21   Pets and People Together, https://petsandpeopletogether.org/.

issues are top reasons people give up their pets.[22] Also, shelters will often include the cost of many health firsts, like their neuter, their vaccinations, or even their microchipping. In fact, many shelters won't let you bring home a dog without neutering them first, to ensure that breeding and overpopulation stops then and there. Shelters often run drives where they lower their adoption fees in order to get more animals in loving homes, so the cost for your pet may be minimal. (Geriatric dogs are often discounted because it's so hard for them to find homes since almost everybody wants a puppy. Of course, saving on adoption fees doesn't necessarily mean that pet care is less expensive throughout the life of your dog, but nobody argues with saving some money up front.)

Shelters also can have puppies as well as purebred dogs available for adoption. Usually, 25 percent of the animals in shelters are purebred![23] That means if you have your heart set on a specific type of dog you can still adopt a shelter pet. Many shelter pets even have full histories available, so you know what kind of animal you're bringing home before you sign the papers. Pets at shelters often undergo a variety of behavioral tests to see how they interact with other dogs, cats, and even small children.

One of the things that can be tough about adopting a shelter dog is their adjustment period once they come home with you. Unfortunately, because of the high levels of overpopulation, shelters around the nation are bursting at their seams.

---

22   "More than 1 Million Households Forced to Give Up Their Beloved Pet Each Year, ASPCA Research Reveals," ASPCA, December 8, 2015, https://www.aspca.org/about-us/press-releases/more-than-1-million -households-forced-to-give-their-beloved-pet-each-year-aspca.

23   "Buyer Beware: The Problem with Puppy Mills and Backyard Breeders," PAWS, https://www.paws.org/resources/puppy-mills/.

This leads to shelters full of too many dogs, dogs who are often dealing with anxiety as a result of not having regular, focused attention, or even enough exercise. It can be scary, living at a shelter. Sometimes it takes a bit for them to emotionally settle and realize that they're safe with you. This adjustment period can last from weeks to months—which sounds long but really isn't in the big scheme of things. Also, not all dogs deal with this. Plenty of them settle in just fine with zero issues whatsoever.[24]

Shelters also will conduct interviews with you and your family to make sure the dog is a good fit. If you rent instead of owning your home, many shelters will contact your landlord to ensure the pet will be allowed. If you already have pets at home, some shelters will require your new dog meet your other dogs to make sure there are no issues. Some shelters will ask questions about your lifestyle and dog care knowledge to get a feel for whether yours is the right home for this dog. Be honest, be patient with people who are simply doing their jobs, and know that these questions are all about making sure the dog gets placed in the best home possible.

Take a few minutes to bust through the misconceptions you may have about shelter animals; I speak from firsthand experience when I say they make incredible pets. More than a million animals are euthanized in shelter and rescue groups each year in the United States, mostly as a result of limited rescue resources.[25] The more pets that are adopted, the fewer that are euthanized. By adopting a shelter animal, you're mak-

---

24 See: Ezra. Our swamp werewolf did way better at home than in the shelter, and adjusted spectacularly well almost immediately.

25 Dr. Sarah Wolff, "Rescue vs. Breeder: How to Find the Right Dog," Companion Pet Hospital, December 1, 2019, https://companionpethospital.com/2019/12/01/rescue-vs-breeder/.

ing room for other pets to have safety, food, love, and maybe (eventually!) a loving home of their own.

Small Rescue Agencies

You may find in your research for a dog that you stumble upon people who run small rescues. These organizations aren't associated with the bigger names, like the ASPCA. Rescues like this are almost entirely private ventures; owners answer only to themselves. Small rescues may have different missions. Often they're focused on a specific breed, size, or type of dog. (Think a small dog only rescue, for example.)

Rescues and shelters both use what's called the foster network, where volunteers give adoptable animals a safe home until they're paired with their forever families. Since many rescues don't have formal space in the same way a shelter does, they may be more dependent on the foster network.

Make sure you do your research and avoid any red flags when using a smaller agency. If a small rescue has a website, give it a good look-see, and make sure the info looks legit. See what their reputation is when you search online. What do the reviews say? Small agencies should be registered as nonprofits, or 501(c)(3)s. This is to ensure you're not buying from a puppy mill posing as a rescue group. Note if they're eager to give their dogs to anyone without any vetting first. Pay attention if their adoption fees are exorbitantly expensive, especially in excess of $500. If they conduct no interviews whatsoever, you should feel a red-flag tingle. If their dogs are only puppies—and especially if they're only purebred puppies—you should ixnay the plan entirely.

Though small rescue agencies may require a little more work to ensure you're adopting from the best place possible, you don't have to strike them entirely from the list simply because they aren't huge. In many cases, you can work directly with the owner to let them know you're looking for specific characteristics. I've adopted from small agencies before; it's how Rupert came to live with us. I told the owner of the agency that I specifically wanted a small-breed puppy under six months old, and boy, did she deliver. Just like with shelter adoption, if you're willing to commit the time, it can be worthwhile.

Breeders

Since this book is written primarily about companion animals, I'm not going to spend a lot of time talking about breeders. Breeders can be the right call for people who are hunting for a very specific breed or a working dog. Buying a dog from a breeder can be a loaded topic nowadays. There is a mindset that all breeders are inherently bad: that they all sell to puppy mills; that they don't health test their pups; that they simply breed their dogs as often as possible without any care in the world. Up front, this isn't true of everyone who breeds dogs.

There are a few things to remember when buying from a breeder. First, depending on where you're located, the animal you purchase must come with a current health certificate signed by a veterinarian. At minimum, you should have access to their veterinary background and any medical needs they may have. If the animal has no evidence of veterinary care (the vaccines and treatments were all administered by the breeder without even a single complete physical exam being performed): red flag. Your pet should be bright-eyed, bushy-tailed, and shiny coated when you interact with them. Dogs who look sick may actually be sick. Some breeds have breed-related health problems, like German Shepherds having terrible hips or Frenchies not being able to breathe due to their flat faces. Do your research! Know what you're getting into!

If you're dealing with a breeder, you should insist on seeing the dog's parents as well as their living facilities. If someone looking to rehome or sell a pet asks you to meet them behind a store, your red-flag meter should be dinging. Most breeders specialize in one or two breeds max, and produce a limited number of litters annually. You may have to wait on a list for a period of months to years before you can bring home your puppy. Puppies being perpetually available are a red flag. Also, exclusivity and high price don't necessarily correlate to quality.

Compared to shelters and small rescues, purchasing a dog from a breeder is going to be a significant financial investment. Usually, a shelter adoption will cost less than $200. Adopting from a small rescue may cost between $250 and $500, but not typically more than that. A breeder will charge thousands of dollars, depending on the type of dog and the dog's lineage. Also, you may not be able to find a dog available in your own state, so you'll have to include the cost of transportation (whether that be via shipping or a road trip to get the dog).

Most importantly, good breeders are dedicated to matching dogs with the right family. Make sure you're working with a reputable breeder if you decide this is the path for you.

Pet Stores, Puppy Mills, and Backyard Breeders

My friends, there is no ethical debate about buying puppies from pet stores. It's simply a big ol' no-no. The prevalence of pet stores that sell puppies is a huge issue, because they have wildly inhumane practices at their core. (Petland is the largest chain of puppy-selling pet stores in the country.) Pet stores get their puppy supplies from what's called a puppy mill. Really, 90 percent of puppies in pet stores come from these puppy mills.[26] Puppy mills are commercial breeding facilities that mass-produce dogs for sale through pet stores or directly to consumers via classified ads or the internet. There are approximately ten thousand puppy mills in the United States, and many puppy mills are not inspected at all, which means there are no verifiable records on their conditions.

In most states, these puppy mills can legally keep hundreds of dogs in cages their entire lives for the sole purpose of producing puppies for sale. These animals are overcrowded; their conditions are unsanitary; they often sit and sleep in their own poop and pee. Animals suffer from dehydration and malnutrition. Sick or dying animals receive minimal veterinary care, if any. Adult animals are bred through their entire lives and then euthanized when no longer "useful." Puppies are often taken from their mothers too soon, leading to behavioral issues. Puppies may have serious health issues once they come home. Puppies in pet stores perpetuate the cycle of puppy mills. Everyone suffers.

The Humane Society keeps a list known as the Horrible Hundred,[27] a collection of known, problematic puppy-breeding or puppy-brokering facilities, in an effort to inform the public about the scope of the puppy mill problem in the United States.

---

26   PAWS, "Buyer Beware."

27   "The Horrible Hundred," The Humane Society of the United States, https://www.humanesociety.org/horriblehundred.

This list is horrifying.[28] Truly, reading it requires an iron stomach. I wish I could rescue all of these babies and show them what love feels like. You'll note that many of the breeders on this list are affiliated with the American Kennel Club (AKC), which is why it is so important you do background research before buying from a breeder.

Similar to the puppy mill is the backyard breeder. Essentially, this is someone who is also motivated by profit when creating puppies for sale. They may seem to be well intentioned, but continuously breeding animals for years to produce for-profit litters jeopardizes the animals' welfare. Backyard breeders usually aren't knowledgeable on responsible breeding; they rarely screen for genetic defects. They choose profit over welfare, and again, everyone suffers. When I first wanted a puppy of my very own as a young adult, I believed many of the untrue stories about dogs from shelters: that they would have behavioral issues, or I wouldn't be able to find a puppy. Roland, my first dog, came from a backyard breeder. He was an amazing dog. He also had a lifelong history of health issues and died young from cancer. Please don't make the same mistakes I made as a nineteen-year-old.

Backyard breeders, puppy mills, and pet stores flood the market with animals, reducing home availability for animals from reputable establishments, shelters, and rescue groups. Please, do right by your future dog and by yourself. Don't support pet stores, puppy mills, or backyard breeders. Dogs deserve better.

---

28   "The Horrible Hundred 2022," The Humane Society of the United States, May 2022, https://www.humanesociety.org/sites/default /files/docs/HSUS_Horrible-Hundred-2022.pdf.

CHAPTER 2

Grooming

D ogs are unquestionably intelligent creatures in their own right, with unique personalities and opinions and different ways of communicating. Of course, they also don't have thumbs, and part of the reason we humans have such a robust relationship with dogs is the ways in which they rely on us (and us on them). Taking care of your dog's body—ensuring that their ears are clean, their nails are trimmed, their fur is brushed, and all of the other myriad ways in which we look out for them—is one of the most important responsibilities we're tasked with as stewards of our pets. These tasks are also different from, say, caring for ourselves or human family members. It takes a little bit of research and a pinch of practice to learn what you need to ensure your dog is cared for appropriately, but it's not so overwhelming that you can't figure it out with my help and regular calendar reminders. (Dog bless those digital sticky notes; they're truly a game changer for the care and upkeep of our furry companions.)

With that, onward.

Collars, Leashes, and Muzzles

Let's start with collars. If you're anything like me, the first thing you want to do when you bring home a new dog is buy brand-new accoutrements. New bowls, new harnesses, and (in my opinion, the most fun!) new collars. Collars might not seem like they're important, but if life happens and you end up with a missing dog, that piece of jewelry might be the difference between your pup coming home to you or not.[29] I can't tell you how many times I've picked up a stray running in traffic[30] and was able to bring them home immediately because they were wearing a collar with tags on.

The two most important things you need to know about your dog's collar is how to fit it and what should be on it. The fit isn't too tough to figure out; make sure it's loose enough to slide over their muzzle and down onto their neck but tight enough that you can't pull the collar back up and over the dog's head without unbuckling it. If you get your dog as a puppy, expect them to outgrow their collar multiple times. Collars that are too tight run the risk of strangulation at worst and plain ol' discomfort at best. They can even embed themselves in your dog's skin, like a metal ring around a growing tree. Sometimes this happens so subtly it's hard to notice, especially when it's covered by fur. Who wants to feel like they're wearing a too-tight button-up every day? Nobody, especially not your dog.

Derek and I don't have kids, so we tend to spoil the heck out of our furry family. Obviously, dogs come into our lives footloose and fancy-free, with bare necks that don't have a hint of jew-

---

29　It's important to note that, for the entirety of their lives, all dogs—no matter the age—are appropriately referred to as "puppy." They do not age out of being puppies. In some ways, the older they get, the more puppy they become. I don't know how to explain this, but anyone you speak to who lives with a dog will likely agree.

30　I don't know how they know I'm the Patron Saint of Lost and Broken Animals, but they do. So much so that I keep a "Lost Dog" kit permanently in my trunk..

elry on. That's what we call collars in our house—jewelry.[31] For us, jewelry comes in the form of very fancy bejeweled leather collars as soon as the dog is old enough to no longer have any projected growth spurts. Our favorite vendor is a small business called Paco Collars, which operates out of their storefront in Berkeley, California. They have some of the best customer service in the biz, and their satisfaction guarantee is top-notch. They'll repair their product no matter what happens to it,[32] and they'll create a memorial bracelet or keychain for you out of the collar when your dog's life comes to its end. Of course, if you're lucky enough to have a shop remotely as cool as Paco Collars near you, shopping local is strongly encouraged!

Fancy leather with shiny stones isn't the only option, though. Plenty of pet stores have a plethora of choices in varying colors and patterns. Some even have collar attachments, like bow ties or flowers. Make sure your pup can't chew those up, but otherwise, go wild.

Of course, while you're probably familiar with just a plain ol' normal collar (looks like a loop around their neck, usually with metal hardware, often called a flat collar), there are other types of collars you can look into, too. A slip collar has a ring at either end; you frequently see it used by professionals at veterinary offices or by people rescuing dogs off the street. It's a little hard to picture, but the length of the collar is dropped through one ring, which forms a noose that slips around the dog's neck. There's no limit on how tight a slip collar can get. They're usually used specifically because they can't be slipped out of, and the pressure against the

---

31   As in, "Come here and let me put your jewelry on!" or, "Naked puppy! You're dry from your bath; time to wear your jewelry again!"

32   Seriously, Roland chewed his collar in half once and they fixed it for us.

throat is distributed evenly around the neck, which moves focused pressure off of the windpipe. Of course, a slip collar can also catch on things and accidentally strangle the dog. They're helpful as emergency backup devices or for very short-term, specific use but really shouldn't be a long-term solution for your pup.

A martingale collar has two loops, one that goes around the dog's neck and one that pulls the collar tight and has a ring attachment for the leash. A martingale collar can be made from leather, fabric, or other materials—technically, a prong collar is a martingale. (But not all martingales are prong collars.) Like a slip collar, a martingale collar tightens when needed, like when your dog pulls or tries to back out of their collar. Martingale collars deter some dogs from pulling and stop them from being able to pull or back out of their collar. Like a slip collar, any collar that tightens should not be left on an unsupervised dog.

"Electronic collars," "shock collars," and "remote collars" are blanket terms for shock collars, which trigger an automatic shock when the dog barks in order to deter the behavior. (Some may have a remote or clicker that instigates the shock for training purposes.) There are recently more "humane" options offered, such as collars that spurt a puff of air or buzz instead of administering an electronic shock. These collars have far more potential for harm than not. Negative training means your dog may associate the shock with rolling in something dead (as intended), or they might connect the shock with a random sound, sight, or texture they're experiencing when they're shocked. Also, who the heck learns well when the discipline is pain? Not me, that's for sure. This is also why I suggest that metal choke chains and prong or pinch collars aren't the best options for companion animals. Pinch collars rely on pain to interact with the animal. Similarly, choke chains are primarily used in training systems that rely on some form of punishment or other noxious stimulus to grab your dog's attention—but nobody learns well when they're being forced into discomfort, and you run the risk of damaging your dog's neck and throat by using those. They definitely aren't recommended by most veterinarians. Once, around Christmas, Derek had a client give up their prong collars permanently after an earnest conversation about why these collars weren't the kind thing for our companion animals. Their dog had a wicked nasty tracheal injury from his collar. We proudly hang that collar on our tree every year in celebration of how education can change lives.

Your dog's collar should have a tag clearly marked with your name (first name optional, last name mandatory) and at least two phone numbers—yours and a backup just in case you can't be reached. Dog forbid you forget to charge your phone on the one day your pup slips out the back gate.

Dog collars should also have room for your dog's vaccination and license tags. Vaccination tags prove that your dog has been appropriately vaccinated for various contagious diseases.[33] The license shows that you have proved to your city that your dog is up-to-date on their vaccinations. Licensing requirements will vary from place to place. In my hometown, we renew our licenses annually and get a break on the fee for neutering our pets. A license will only be issued if we can prove our pets have been vaccinated for the specified period. Nothing about this is complex; it's just a few levels of bureaucracy to hop through. Fabulously, ensuring that your pet is licensed will usually also create a record at the local level, just in case your pet gets out and is brought to animal control.

---

33   More on this in the health chapter (chapter 6).

Just like collars, leashes come in a ton of options. We get ours from Paco Collars, too, and I use a hands-free belt to walk the pack. The standard length is a six-foot leash, though they're typically available between four and eight feet. Leashes are usually made out of nylon or leather and some may have reflective striping on them to help you be better seen when out walking in public. Adjustable-length leashes exist, usually with the addition or removal of loops to the lead. This can be helpful if you're training in a way that requires your dog to be very close to your heels. Most leashes are built for the purpose of attaching to one dog, but double leads do exist.

I strongly suggest that you invest in a separate leash specifically for the car. This leash will have an adaptor that slides into the seat belt connection, which keeps your dog safe while you drive and especially in case of a car accident. Another safety option is to crate your dogs inside the vehicle while traveling. Horror stories abound of dogs being injured in accidents because they literally flew through the air after impact, or of them slipping out of cars after an accident and being hit by other vehicles whose drivers weren't expecting a dog on the road. We leave the seat-belt leashes in the car for easy access. Non–seat belt designs, long leads, or leashing your dog loose in the back of a truck is actively dangerous and often leads to injured or dead dogs. Just spend the money. You're already all in.

The biggest thing to avoid is retractable leashes with thin, rope cords. They can cause severe burns, deep cuts, entanglement, and—again—strangulation. It can even cause amputation to limbs and fingers of dogs and their owners. Grabbing the cord portion of the leash (especially while it's being pulled on from the other end) significantly increases the chance of injury. If you have a weak stomach, I don't recommend the

Google search, but if you want to be scared off of retractable leashes forever, the truth is out there.

Leashes save lives. Having your dog on a leash is the number one way to keep your dog from behaving badly or having bad behavior perpetrated upon them.

You might not think of a harness as a type of leash, but it does fall into the same category. Many dogs benefit from a harness because it gives their owner more control. Harnesses are also thought to be more comfy and easier for dogs to adjust to than a plain ol' collar. Most harnesses clip on the front and the back, and you'll figure out which options work best for you and your dog. (All of our dogs have harnesses, and we clip on the back while walking.)

Some owners pair harnesses with head halters, which are commonly used as an alternative to neck control collars. The head halter has a strap that encircles your dog's muzzle. Where their nose goes, their body follows. These head halters minimize issues associated with pulling but can be difficult (if not entirely impossible) for some dogs to adjust to. Training and patience are key here. The muzzle for a head halter goes over and around their snout but doesn't function as a muzzle or to prevent biting. Head halters may also help control barking as well as turning your dog's head away from any stimulus that gets them worked up, but if you know your pet has an aggression problem then a muzzle will be more suitable for the prevention of biting.

Just like everything else I've talked about in this chapter, muzzles can be useful. Muzzles have a stigma associated with them, but they're a valuable safety tool to keep dogs and people safe. The type of muzzle that's appropriate is going to depend on the circumstance, so if you think your dog might need a muzzle, chatting with a veterinarian—especially a veterinary behaviorist—is your best call.

Muzzles that have a basket weave pattern in their design allow dogs to open their mouths comfortably for panting, drinking water, and even eating small treats. Muzzles that hold your dog's mouth closed can cause overheating in as little as fifteen minutes. Occlusion muzzles are more like a straitjacket that wraps around your dog's mouth, keeping it closed. These can lead to dangerous health situations and should be avoided. Also, dogs who have short snouts (think Pugs or Bulldogs) have muzzle options, too. Short-snout muzzles look like masks made out of breathable mesh. Some even have an eyehole design so dogs can see more clearly when wearing them. Again, muzzles can be a useful tool, but talking with your veterinarian to make sure you select one that doesn't hurt your dog is a necessity.

Of course, if your dog is a brand-new puppy or a stray who has never worn a collar or walked on a leash before, they might express discomfort with this weird new jangly thing around their neck. They might try to rub their faces on the ground or scratch at it. Don't worry. I promise they'll eventually get used to it, especially if you give them lots of positive reinforcement.[34] Eventually they'll forget all about it, except for when you take it off before baths or prolonged periods in the crate. Then they'll probably want a good sniff and a quick zoom around the house.

Ultimately, the collar, leash, and harness are important investments, and not just for their safekeeping or because they make dogs fashionable as heck. A collar with tags on it means your dog is officially part of your family—a family that will do anything to keep them safe and protected. It's kind of a big deal.

---

34   Neck scratches and treats always work!

Baths

Look, y'all, I'm gonna tell you something straight out of the veterinarian's mouth and you're not gonna like it: dogs are self-cleaning. I know, but it's true. The average dog—taking a consistent flea preventative and with no underlying medical conditions—does not actually need a bath. I understand that we humans bathe regularly and we expect dogs to live up to those same standards, but the reality is that our furry friends, uh, aren't humans. What can I say?

Okay, yes, the number of needed baths changes if your dog thinks of Eau de Dead Lizard as perfume or is partial to a good roll around on the stink of a dead earthworm.[35] There are other exceptions to the "self-cleaning dog" rule— allergies, an underlying skin condition, and coat type. Longer coats make for more primping. Some dogs require medicated shampoo. Those specifics are something your veterinarian can help you make decisions about. But generally speaking, bathing your dog once a week (or bringing them to the groomer that often) is probably overkill. It's also unlikely to prevent or address most skin conditions when used as the sole solution.

If, however, your pooch does need a bath and you decide to do it yourself, invest in treats. Smear peanut butter or cheese along the back of the bathtub to keep your pup distracted while you lather them up. (Make sure you buy treats without any xylitol in the ingredients list; it's a sugar-free sweetener added to some food that's deadly to dogs. And look to avoid

---

35   I'm convinced dogs don't understand why we don't appreciate the same gross smells, and talk smack about how we simply don't have "sensitive enough noses" to appreciate the smells they do.

birch sugar as well—it's just a prettier name for xylitol.) You can also freeze chicken broth solid in a paper cup for your dog to lick. Also, dog shampoo is a necessity, not an option. The stuff humans use isn't best suited for dog skin.

Before you begin, make sure the water is at a lukewarm temperature—not cool enough to be cold, but just warm enough to feel good. Test it against the inside of your wrist before bath time commences! I've found that a lot of dogs[36] are scared of the loud noise of the faucet, so I fill the tub to about tummy height and use a plastic cup for wetting and rinsing. Never glass. Trust me that when glass goes wrong in a bathtub, it goes *really* wrong. A detachable showerhead is useful here. Also, a soft washcloth can be used to clean your dog's muzzle and around their eyes so you're not pouring water or pushing chemicals in their ears and up their nose.

Some humans bring their dogs to see a groomer instead of doing the work themselves, which is perfectly fine so long as you do the research to find a qualified salon. Make sure that the groomer is licensed, with both experience and training, before you drop your pup off with them. Most of the time, seeing a groomer means a car trip, though there is an increasing number of mobile groomers who will make the trip to see you. This is a great option for dogs who are afraid of the car or who might not be socialized enough to hang out with other pets.[37] Using a groomer is more expensive than doing the work yourself, but not having to deal with a wet dog can be worth every

---

36 Smaller dogs; big ones tend to care less.

37 No judgment here—Rupert was a pandemic puppy, and getting him salon-ready took months of training. Harper, Dog rest her soul, was ill-behaved from utero and could never be trusted around other dogs besides Roland.

penny. Because of their intimate experiences with your dog's body, groomers are sometimes the front line for detecting ear and skin problems and suggesting clients bring their pet for a veterinary visit.

Oh, and drying them off? Expect a good wet shake that manages to fling water all over everything. If you're speedy, you can get a quick rubdown in before they do that, but you have to *move* to do it. I strongly suggest you wear your junky house clothes for this chore, too. Usually, I bathe my dogs in a swimsuit or my underwear, and I fully expect to take a shower after to rinse the smell of wet dog off of me.

Again, big dogs will sometimes put up with an outside bath where the baptism occurs via hose, but make sure your water and the outside temperature aren't too cold before doing this.

Hands down, though, the best parts of a bath are the "zoomies" that come afterward. Have you ever seen a video of a dog absolutely losing their mind, running full tilt through the house, ricocheting off the furniture and barking their fool heads off? Welcome to the zoomies, my friend, population: your dog. Nobody knows the scientific reason for why dogs go bonkers after a bath, but it is an absolute joy to experience and worth the sore back from bathing them yourself.

Nail Trims

No joke, nail trims are the main reason why I pay a groomer to take care of my dogs. It's a regular dog maintenance task that is absolutely necessary for keeping your dogs healthy, but I hate doing it with a passion and would so much rather that someone else be the bad guy, since my dogs don't like it much, either. Of course, the vast majority of dogs will eventually tolerate nail trims just fine with gentle and diligent buildup to normalizing the chore. No shame if that's not your game, but no need to be scared off attempting to do something you might be able to accomplish on your own.

Nails should be trimmed every two to six weeks, but you absolutely shouldn't wait longer than that—even for puppies. If you can hear your dog's nails clicking on the tile, they're already too long.

Dog toenails grow in a curve, like a crescent. This is different from the way human nails grow. If your dog's toenails get too long, it can cause their toes to splay and twist and can actually affect the way they walk, causing pain and discomfort in the short term and even having potential long-term effects like muscle strain; they can even grow all the way around in a semi- or full circle, embedding themselves into the paw pad. It's a gnarly injury that no dog should suffer.

Inside their toenail is an incredibly sensitive cuticle containing the blood vessel and nerves that run through your dog's nail. This is called the quick. As dogs' nails grow longer, the quick grows, too, which means it becomes easier to accidentally trim while cutting their nails. When you trim the quick it bleeds like heck, and it hurts. (It feels like when you accidentally tear off your own fingernail too short!) It's a bad time for everybody involved and there is nothing like the look of absolute betrayal when you nip the quick during a nail trim.

Fortunately, regular nail trims mean that the quick recedes and stays short. You can actually see the quick in your dog's nails if you look. It's the little pink line in the center of the white. Another reason I pay a groomer for nail trims is because I am cursed with dogs who have black nails. It's much more challenging to see the quick when you've got a dog who has dark nails. It can be done, but you just have to trim slowly and only trim back a little bit at a time. As you trim little segments of nail, you'll find the pulp, which is located just before the quick. The pulp is soft tissue that's black and circular. So when you see the black circle in the middle of the cut nail it's time to stop!

Of course, even groomers sometimes accidentally nick the quick.[38] It stings. So I recommend you keep styptic powder called Kwik Stop on hand to stop the bleeding quickly. Yes, you will feel an excessive amount of guilt any time you do this. Yes, your dog will learn to make their best sad face and wheedle treats out of you as an apology. (And it's a common reason dogs hate nail trims.)

A good trick for trimming nails at home is to bend your dog's paws backward (the way they bend naturally, toward their tail) instead of forward (like when shaking paws with someone). Although it may look a little odd, it's significantly more comfortable for your pup to be in this position.[39] A groomer typically uses dog clippers with a sharp cutting blade for nail trims, following up with a Dremel to file down any rough spots. The loud sound from the Dremel might startle your dog, but it won't hurt them—it's like a nail file. Sometimes, dogs who are too nervous to have their nails trimmed or Dremeled might benefit from using a scratch pad. This pad has an emory board attached, which allows the dog to file their own nails down. Using the scratch pad requires patience and training, but it shouldn't be excluded as an option.

The best thing you can do for your dog is start them with regular nail trims when they're young so they become accustomed to the experience and don't find it stressful. Gentle

---

38   Say that ten times fast. "Nick the quick."

39   Think about the way a farrier holds a horse's leg the way they do when applying shoes. Way more comfy.

handling of their paws in calm moments is also integral for normalization. Also, I cannot understate how important treats are as bribery through the training process. The direct path to most dogs' hearts is through their stomach and knowing that from the start will make everybody's lives easier. In fact, just like people, dogs are motivated by rewards and kindness. If you remember that from the start, everyone will be happier.

Ear Cleaning

Dogs' ears, like their skin, don't need regular cleaning unless there's a specific medical need, like an active infection or an underlying chronic skin condition—both of which will necessitate guidance from your vet.[40] In fact, ear canals are technically specialized skin, so they can be treated as one region within the general skin category. Cleaning earwax out can be okay if owners insist, but it isn't strictly medically necessary and should happen at *most* once a week in the absence of a medical need.

Taking care of the cleaning part at home when there's no health problems going on isn't too tough, though. Most dogs strongly believe that cold, wet stuff shouldn't be in their ears.[41] I strongly believe that dogs think the only thing making an ear cleaning worth it is the satisfaction of a headshake that covers us in whatever goop we used for said cleaning. Also, the longer

---

40 Keep in mind that ear infections can sometimes be a sign of larger skin infections, too, not just ear problems. If things look funky—ears that are red or tender to the touch or have that very particular muddy stink—that likely means they're infected and it's probably worth a visit to the vet to get things checked out.

41 Other dogs' noses notwithstanding.

you put it off, the better your dog can avoid listening when you ask them to do something they don't want to, like, say, "stop harassing the cat" or "please don't make that disgusting sound while licking your butt."

Dog ears should be cleaned using a mild ear cleanser, preferably one recommended by your veterinarian. You'll need to be careful about what's in the cleanser, because that which smells good to our human noses can be toxic to our dogs. Lavender, eucalyptus, and tea-tree oil are all bad for dogs. Borax, vinegar, peroxide, rubbing alcohol, salt water, and other caustics are commonly used by people who think they're a safe option. They aren't. In our house, we only use veterinary-recommended products, usually ones we purchase during regular checkups.

The nice thing about your dog's ears is that their ear canals are shaped like an L, with the eardrum at the far end of the bottom of the L. That means it's pretty hard to hurt the delicate parts deep inside. You basically can't get a Q-tip (which you shouldn't be using here anyways[42]) into that L unless you're doing something very wrong.

For an ear cleaning, I make sure I have a towel nearby—not for wiping anything up, but for holding up like a shield after my dogs inevitably shake their heads and send ear cleanser spattering everything. Some people might want to use a soaked cotton ball or cotton pad[43] for cleanser application, to help give a good swipe around the skin of their dog's ears nearer to their ear canal, where the folds start and the fur stops. Derek has unfortunately found cotton balls in dog's ear canals weeks to months after ear cleanings (even those performed by pro-

---

42 Or in your ears, either.

43 Soft only, not the kind used for exfoliation.

fessionals!), so if you can get away with not using something you have to remember to remove after the fact all the better. You definitely don't want to pack any foreign objects into your dog's ears, and cotton balls count as foreign.

With the medication in my dog's ear, I give a good *squish, squish, squish* at the base of their ear to get everything soaked. Like I said, I skip the cotton ball and just fill the ear canal with the cleanser, but I never skip the squishing. The squish feels good—it's the cleanser that feels funky. Then, when everything is good and sopping, I let them shake their head. (This is where the towel comes in.) Repeat as needed.

If your dog has an ear infection and you're using medicated cleansers or actual medication, you may notice that your dog has black or green stuff coming out of their ears while cleaning them. This should go away with proper treatment. If you notice that (or blood, or that aforementioned awful smell!), see your veterinarian for a prescription to help. Of course, many dogs have dark brown or black ear gunk as part of their normal body function. If you're worried, follow up with your vet.

I admit that I kinda love this chore. There's a satisfaction in it that you can't find anywhere else. I know maybe that makes me weird, but I'll take it.

Toothbrushing

Anyone who has ever seen a picture of the skull of a human child with their adult teeth exposed below the little-kid teeth that will fall out knows that teeth are flipping weird. If you haven't seen this, go ahead and Google.[44] I'll wait. . . . Done? Yeah, I can tell—I can hear you screaming from here. Teeth, man. Ew.

---

44   "Child skull adult teeth" will get you what I'm talkin' about.

Teeth are exactly as weird for dogs. Puppies have puppy teeth, which they lose the same way humans do. I mean, I've never tied a string around a puppy tooth and slammed a door to pull it out, but you get the idea.[45] Similarly to humans, newborn puppies are born without teeth. They go through a teething stage at around three weeks old, and then they start to lose their puppy teeth by three to four months old.

A lot of times they'll simply swallow their puppy teeth. Sometimes it might get stuck in a toy or you'll find it on the ground later. This is totally normal. It's also normal for their puppy teeth to be very sharp compared to their adult teeth. This stage is a great time for you to socialize them by touching their mouth, gently and without causing stress, around the outside, as well as inside, on their teeth and gums. This will prep them for having their teeth brushed. Also, puppies have a very specific mouth smell while teething. I call it coffee breath, and kinda like the smell of an ear infection, it's impossible to explain unless you've smelled it firsthand. On the bright side, puppy coffee breath is way better than ear infection stink.

Yup, like humans, dogs are supposed to brush their teeth, too. Or rather, we're supposed to brush their teeth for them, since they don't have thumbs. It's easy enough. Swap human toothpaste with dog toothpaste, but keep the same toothbrush. (Soft bristled, though. Kid's toothbrushes work best.) Focus on brushing the outside of their teeth and yes, brushing daily is the goal. (Derek says that if we humans don't brush their teeth at least three times a week minimum we shouldn't even bother. That's how frequently it needs to be done to help cut back on plaque, tartar, gum disease, and tooth decay.) Brushing won't remove visible tartar or calculus, though; once you see a dis-

---

45   I really hope I don't have to tell you this is NOT RECOMMENDED.

coloration on your dog's teeth, it's only going to come off with a visit to the vet and a dental. Brushing is purely preventative!

If your dog absolutely will not let you brush their teeth—or if it's something you simply can't do, for whatever reason—an alternative to an actual toothbrush is to offer them Greenies or another type of dental chew to accomplish the same goal of fighting plaque. Some people say that bones work well for this, but since chewing on bones comes with a trade-off of possibly breaking their teeth, causing a gastrointestinal foreign body, or other complications, it's a treat I skip. I don't have the patience or motor skills to brush my pack's teeth regularly, so my dogs get regular dates with Greenies and full annual dentals instead.

Full Dental

A full dental is not a substitute for regular toothbrushing, nor vice versa. Even if you're regularly brushing your dog's teeth, they should also be getting a full dental every year or so. This is preferable from the time your dog is a year old but definitely should be happening by the time your dog is five or so. A full dental means a trip to the vet, where your dog will be given anesthesia that conks them out completely. Once your dog is anesthetized, the vet and their technicians use dental instruments to scrape plaque off your dog's teeth and away from below their gumline, the same way your dentist does.[46]

Anesthesia during a full dental is completely safe when administered by a responsible licensed veterinarian and it's also absolutely imperative. Even a dog who has their teeth brushed

---

46   If you are lucky enough to have dental insurance in this capitalist hellscape.

regularly is going to find the process of having their teeth cleaned thoroughly strange, and some of the instruments necessary to effectively clean your dog's teeth might accidentally hurt their mouth if they're moving around. Anesthesia means no wiggling. Full anesthesia makes the dental safer and more effective.

Some veterinary practices advertise "nonanesthetic dental procedures," but what they don't tell you is that no anesthesia means someone is restraining your dog while holding open their mouth. Not only is this terrifying for your pet, but it also means the vet can't get below your dog's gums, where the root of tooth decay usually lives. Part of why an annual dental is so important is because a regular toothbrush can't reach the parts of the tooth below the gumline. The yellowish-orange discoloration you see on dog's teeth is a buildup of plaque, which houses bacteria—something that's common, especially as your dog ages. However, most of the diseases that affect your dog's health and teeth live below their gumline, so plaque buildup might be normal, but it's still something we want to avoid. Wolves don't get dentals, sure—but they suffer the pain and other complications of dental infections as a result.

In the same way that a good vet will anesthetize your dog for their dental, they'll also use an on-site X-ray machine to take pictures of your dog's tooth roots and jawbones during their dental cleaning. Like with humans, you're only getting half the story without good pictures of what's going on beneath their skin and below their gums.

Typically, when your dog is younger you won't have to worry about them needing to get teeth pulled. This isn't true for every dog. Smaller dogs, like Rupert, and older dogs, like Ezra, usually end up having a few teeth pulled. In fact, Rupert had something called retained deciduous canines, where his adult canines came in, but his puppy canines hadn't fallen out. Retained deciduous teeth can cause crowding, discomfort, or even infection, so we had his extra teeth pulled. Ezra came to us from the shelter with such an awful set of teeth that I had to sign a waiver promising to bring him to a dentist before I could adopt him. This is part of why he only has seven teeth left—and realistically, he'll probably have lost the rest by the time you read this.[47] Fortunately, no teeth is more comfortable than infected teeth.

The fancy word for this tooth pulling is "extraction." Pulling teeth is just the cost of doing business, and the alternative is (at minimum) stinky dog breath and yellow teeth. More likely, not taking care of your dog's teeth will lead to dental disease, pain, the risk of a broken jaw, abscesses, and inflammation. Nobody likes that.

Anal Gland Expression

If you just did a double take after reading that heading, you're probably not alone. I've thus far covered your dog's front end. There's a surprising amount you have to know about their back end to be a good dog owner.

Dogs identify each other by their butts. The way they smell is like a personal identification number, which is why they give the rear end a good sniff whenever they meet someone new (or greet someone they've already met). It's also why they sniff poop if they're out and about on a walk. They get a ton of information from what comes out of their backsides.

---

47   Between the first draft of this book and the final, he lost five more teeth. Wasn't kidding.

Dogs have two small glands (or sacs) on their derrière, both of which produce an excretion with a scent that tells other dogs important facts, like their sex, health, and approximate age. These glands are naturally emptied (or expressed) by the process of a normal poop in most dogs. (And what comes out of them has a huge range for what's considered "normal," from light brown liquid to chalky toothpaste colored. Aren't butts fun?)

Sometimes, if your dog has diarrhea, or is constipated, or dehydrated, or has any skin conditions, their anal glands can become impacted—another fancy word, this one basically meaning "backed up." If those glands are blocked up for too long, they can become infected and form an abscess—a painful pocket of pus. So, if your dog starts scooting their butt on the floor or licking at their rear end, it might be time to have someone express their anal glands.[48] I find that the slurping sounds of them licking at themselves drives me to the brink of absolutely losing it. I like it when they drag their butt on the ground even less.

Much like with everything else in this chapter, you can do the expression yourself (unless your dog is markedly impacted or has an abscess). Alternatively, you can bring your dog to the vet (or sometimes a groomer) to have it done. There's an internal method and an external method, and a verbal description would absolutely not do justice to the process. This is one that you're just going to have to see for yourself. Trust me when I say it's worth a demonstration from someone who knows what they're doing. It is worth every single penny in

---

48   This might also be a sign of fecal parasites, so it's worth a trip to the vet to differentiate.

extra tips given to vet techs or groomers who handle this part of caring for my dogs.

It's, uh, never comfortable to have someone squeeze that particular bit of your anatomy, especially if it's already feeling tender. Dogs don't always love this, and can you blame them? Once you've figured out how to do this after a clear demonstration, I suggest performing the process either outside or in the bathtub. Most importantly, make sure to stay out of the line of fire.

Brushing Your Dog

I will not fault you if you need to step away from this book for a moment and grab a sip of water. As a kid, I did not know that anal sac discussion would be such a large part of my adulthood, but then, who is capable of picturing what it's like to be a grown-up when you don't have to pay bills, file taxes, and express your dog's anal glands?

Let's talk about something a little more pleasant: brushing your dog's fur. This chore, at least, is probably one that doesn't seem quite so surprising. How frequently you brush depends on your dog's fur type. Rupert, a short-haired Rat Terrier, pretty much doesn't need to be brushed, or only very casually brushed once every couple of days. Sebastian, a very fluffy Papillon mix, needs a thorough brush and haircut at the groomer's every three weeks or so. Brushing is absolutely something a groomer can do, too. Some dogs have more complex needs because of the kind of dog they are. Not everybody lives in tropical Florida like my pack. Some dogs live in snow and have undercoats that have to be blown out when the seasons change. It's a complicated thing, and as usual, having this conversation with your veterinarian is the right call. I cannot overstate how important it's going to be to have a veterinarian as part of your life after you get a dog. I'm not saying I married a veterinarian because of my love of dogs, but I'm not *not* saying it, either.

While dogs with different fur types will be brushed differently, there are some general rules for every dog. First, make sure to brush in the direction of your dog's hair growth. (Same for toweling dogs off dry, especially if they have short fur. Short-coated dogs can end up with their fur driven into their skin like tiny daggers if you aren't careful.) Second, don't use too much pressure when brushing. Third, choose the right brush for the fur or hair type. The big trick is picking the right brush for the fur, really. Most pet stores will sell "shedding blades," which cut back on leaving fur all over the place or getting matted up.

Finally, be patient! Like with most grooming tasks, being brushed starts out feeling funky, but it can feel really nice if your dog is in the right mood or has been socialized to view brushing as a fun way to spend time with their human. It's superrelaxing, it might make them a little bit sleepy, and it can be a great bonding experience with the right dog.

Clothes

I deeply regret that I have never owned a dog who enjoys wearing clothes. I mean, from a medical standpoint, dogs wearing clothes is almost completely unnecessary. From a style standpoint, dogs look hella good no matter what they wear.

As always, there are exceptions. There are some medical conditions where clothes are necessary for your dog, and certain breeds might need clothes, specifically in nonpigmented-skin areas. (Though I will tell you now that dogs can wear sunscreen to protect their skin, too, especially if they love to sunbathe! Just make sure to use dog-safe sunscreen.)

If you are blessed with a dog who enjoys clothing, there are some general rules:

1. Dogs have to be able to potty without soiling themselves, because nobody likes wearing pee-covered clothes all day. Clothing design will vary depending on your dog's external genitalia, so make sure you match the right crotch design to your dog's needs.
2. Dog clothes should be laundered regularly, especially if they're wearing them regularly. Use a detergent with minimal or no scents for this.
3. Be very careful about wrapping any kind of clothing around a limb and holding it in place with tension. It is scarily easy to cut off circulation to paws, tails, or ears and cause serious injury. Hair ties, rubber bands, and bandages can all cause significant damage in this realm.
4. Finally, remember that if you're uncomfortable—if you're too hot, too cold, whatever—your dog probably is, too.

Besides that, there are all kinds of clothes for your dog. I've seen dogs in hats, helmets, jackets, sweaters, pajamas—you name it. TikTok is truly a gift for outfitted pooches. There are even special kinds of clothes used for specific reasons. Have you ever heard of a Thunder Jacket? That's a jacket that wraps dogs up nice and firm like a hug to make them calmer if they're feeling anxious.[49]

---

49   Great for fireworks!

There are booties for their feet that they can wear in the snow or on hot asphalt. Yes, their paws can become accustomed to an enormous range of environments, but dogs are unfortunately still mortal. Heck, there's even stuff made specifically for when dogs get old. There are toe grips and little stickers that stick on to paw pads to help with traction when dogs get arthritis in their hips. Some dogs stop being able to stand up on their own when the arthritis sets in, so there are also slings dogs can wear so humans have help lifting them up.

I, for one, am of the opinion that there is no dog out there who wouldn't look killer in a custom denim jacket with their name airbrushed on the back. No question. Add some rhinestones and you cannot tell me that dog isn't living their best life. I only regret that my pack refuses. Any attempt to put them in clothes leads to outright rebellion. One day, in this lifetime, I will have a dog who lets me dress them up, though. I'm manifesting it right now.[50]

---

50 Ezra does have a battle jacket he'll suffer through if he gets enough love after, but he doesn't *enjoy* the process. I want a dog who likes the clothes, darn it.

CHAPTER 3

Feeding

If dogs had opposable thumbs, I am almost positive that they would spend exactly as much time as we humans do standing in the kitchen, fridge door thrown wide open, basking in the cold white light, absolutely marveling at the absolute excess of options available. For dogs, though, food can be summed up quite succinctly as, *I'm hungry. Again. Still.* Since they're entrusted to our care, we have to take a little more time to figure out the details before filling their bellies. You will quickly learn that puppies can devour their own weight several times a day, and the nutrients in those morsels are important.

Mealtime Basics

Ahh, mealtime. The who, what, where, when, sit, and stay, as it were? My pack typically eats out of stainless-steel bowls or puzzle feeders placed on the floor,[51] but I did a ton of research as to the cost, style, safety, durability, and how easy the bowls were to clean before settling on the ones I did. I counted out plastic, as it's not usually great for dogs because they can chew on it. Also, I am clumsy and will unquestionably drop anything ceramic or otherwise breakable, which then shatters. Stainless steel is dishwasher safe, and though I don't encourage the dogs

---

51   Technically, inside their crates—and each dog has a separate crate.

licking the bowls while they're being loaded, I also don't necessarily dissuade them, because I am a sucker for keeping my pups happy.[52]

My pack's bowls are on the floor specifically because none of them are very big, but some tall dogs eat from elevated bowls because it's more comfortable for them (this helps for dogs who might have sore necks or backs, too!). My pack eats in their crates because Bashi is food aggressive and the crate protects everyone from him and him from himself. Also, it encourages good behavior and a positive association with the crate for crate training.

Puzzle feeders are another option for dogs and can be made of fabric or plastic. These are fun for challenging your dog's brain and giving them a bit of mental stimulation, but dogs shouldn't be left alone with them due to the materials they're made from. Also, not every dog will enjoy the process of a bowl that makes them work for their dinner. Any time I pull the feeders out, Rupert and Bashi are thrilled and Ezra refuses the meal out of staunch obstinance. Your mileage, as always, may vary.

Once you figure out the whole bowl thing, you have to decide on the type of dog food you'll be feeding your pooch. Owning a dog means unintentionally opting into more unsolicited advice about dog food than you could have ever imagined, so let's stick to the basics.

First, avoid grain-free foods. They have been linked to heart disease that can shorten your pet's life span, and the FDA is currently investigating.[53] Grain-free dog foods are com-

---

52 Or maybe just a sucker.

53 "The Link Between Grain-Free Pet Foods and Canine Heart Disease," Jacksonville Community Pet Clinic, April 22, 2021, https:// mycommunitypetclinic.com/the-link-between-grain-free-pet-foods -and-canine-heart-disease/

monly advertised by boutique or smaller brands as being preferable due to their ingredients (or lack therof). They aren't.

In fact, when picking who makes the food you feed your dog, stick with the Big Five brands: Eukanuba, Hill's, IAMS, Purina, and Royal Canin. These companies produce the safest options for your dog because their foods are formulated by veterinary nutritionists and meet AAFCO standards. No, I didn't just quack at you like a duck. AAFCO stands for the Association of American Feed Control Officials; they're an organization that helps regulate animal feeds. The other nice thing about eating food from a big company is that you're easily able to trace the food back to the producer if problems arise, like contamination or toxicity in a batch that might make dogs sick. It doesn't happen often, but it can happen.

Besides picking the manufacturer of your dog's food, you also need to select the life-stage-appropriate diet for them. This is simpler than it sounds. Basically, read the labels on the food and make sure it matches up with where your dog is in their life. Ezra eats a diet formulated for senior dogs; Rupert just moved away from puppy food and onto the same diet Bashi eats.

Your dog's primary nutrition should come from a high-quality, balanced, and complete canine-specific diet. Some dog owners talk about home-cooked diets, raw diets, or boutique diets, but they run into trouble because those meals usually aren't balanced with all the nutrients and vitamins dogs actually need to be healthy. Don't get me wrong, humans *can* feed their dogs that way, but they're most successful if they work with their vet and a veterinary nutritionist (which is a veterinarian with additional specialized schooling focused on pet nutrition, in the same way that human doctors specialize in specific systems by becoming cardiologists, neurologists, or oncologists).

Once you get those details figured out, you pretty much just have to read the labels to see recommendations for how much food dogs are fed per meal. Puppies are a little bit different than older dogs because they need to eat at least three times a day since they're tiny and burning through those calories quickly as they grow like weeds. They may even need more than three meals a day. (Kind of like young humans.) Similarly, smaller breeds ideally need more meals to maintain even blood sugar through the day. No dog at any age should eat fewer than two times a day. I know some people only feed their dogs once a day, and I just want to shake those people. Have they never been hangry before?

Eating Poop

Aside from, y'know, dog food, you may find that your dog sometimes eats poop.[54] In fancy medical terms, this is called coprophagia. Grossly, this is a pretty normal puppy behavior. Puppies learn about the world by exploring using all of their senses, their sense of taste included. Most puppies outgrow the behavior of eating poop (especially if you're providing the proper guidance and positive reinforcement). You can't eat what's not there, so restricting access and getting rid of poop as quickly as you can is a good call.[55] This is also where training a "leave it" or "drop it" command comes in handy.

---

54 Their own and poop from other pets. Like, say, the litter box. Insert puking emoji here. Also used tampons and underwear that's been worn. Dogs are disgusting.

55 We have a gate that keeps the dogs away from the litter box for a reason.

Dogs who are bored, stressed, anxious, or desperate for attention may find comfort in coprophagia. Make sure your pup is having their exercise needs met and their brains enriched. This means lots of playtime! Also, there's a hypothesis (but no proof) that a dog whose diet is lacking in various nutrients may seek out what's missing in their poop. This is where that high-quality, well-balanced diet I was talking about comes into play.

Ultimately, eating poop is absolutely rancid but not the weirdest thing in the dog world. If you have serious concerns and can't seem to address the behavior, (say it with me!) chat with your vet.

Eating Grass

Less gross but still pretty yucky (especially if you've ever stepped barefoot on a regurgitated pile of it) is when your dog eats grass. You'll commonly hear that dogs eat grass when their tummy is upset. Some dogs chow down on grass and puke shortly thereafter. It can sometimes turn into a chicken or the egg problem: Does the dog eat grass and vomit to soothe an upset stomach, or do they get an upset tummy and puke because they ate grass?

This one also doesn't have a clear answer. Again, dogs may eat grass because they're exploring the world using their mouths. They may be seeking attention, or pursuing the tasty snack because it's specifically forbidden. There is some evidence that grass eating may again be associated with dietary deficiencies, so making sure you have that high-quality, well-balanced diet remains important, dang it.

Unlike coprophagia, there have been some studies conducted on eating grass.[56] One of these studies concluded that dogs don't eat grass to make themselves puke. It also found that younger dogs were more likely to snack on grass than older dogs, and that it seems to be influenced by how hungry they are (eating a meal led to less grass eating). Another study found that dogs with GI upset in their large intestines were less likely to eat grass, but we still don't have answers about dogs with GI upset in their stomach or small intestines.

Ultimately, we don't exactly know why dogs eat grass. We just know that they do; it's a fairly normal dog behavior. Of course, dogs may ingest grass that's been treated with pesticides or grass that has the poop of other animals in it, leading to parasite exposure. As usual, keep an eye on your dog and know that training and access are also methods for control here. To minimize the behavior, you can avoid grassy areas and only hang out in grass after a meal, when they have a full tummy.

I think I've mentioned it before, but dogs are frickin' weird.

Gettin' High

Let's talk about cannabis, also known as marijuana or weed. Access to this medication/drug has become more ubiquitous in the United States as states and the federal government have moved toward legalization. (I thought seriously about making a grass pun given the previous section before I realized nobody calls it grass anymore. Did they ever? I'm genuinely not sure.) Long story short, dogs have a tendency to get themselves into cannabis of all shapes and forms. Some dogs even seek out the

---

56   Wailani Sung, "Why Do Dogs Eat Grass?," PetMD, August 31, 2021, https://www.petmd.com/dog/wellness/evr_dg_eating_grass.

ash. We're not sure if they recognize the correlation between cannabis and feeling *fine* for the next few hours, but I wouldn't be surprised if that was the case.

In fact, a high dog looks remarkably similar to a high human. Classic signs include bobblehead movements and wobbly gait. Some dogs may dribble urine or pee more than usual. Many dogs will startle easily when medicated. And, of course, cannabis-intoxicated dogs will frequently show signs of sedation, including being flat-out asleep or unrousable if they've gotten into a fair amount.

Cannabis intoxication rarely requires hospitalization and doesn't cause death or long-term complications in your dog. It's not an uncommon experience, given how prone they are to seeking it out. (One time, a dog I was fostering managed to find a tiny bit of brownie in a zipped-up backpack.) Classic signs of cannabis intoxication may mimic other neurological issues, though, so it's worth bringing your pooch to the vet for a checkup if you think they might have snuck into your stash.

Weight

Maintaining an ideal weight for your dog is the best way to keep them alive and healthy for longer than their already way-too-short life-spans. Essentially, an "ideal weight" just means that we need to pay attention to our dogs and their bodies—their *actual* bodies, not what they're "supposed" to look like because of their breed. Just like with every human, there's a different ideal weight for every individual dog. Two dogs of the same body weight and breed may require very different amounts of the same food to maintain their healthy body weight.

What does a healthy weight look like? Good question!

Some dogs have big barrel chests and some dogs naturally have rolls and rolls of excess skin, so assessing those details doesn't really work as a good way to judge what's healthy. A healthy weight is when you can feel your dog's ribs but not see them (and when their belly is narrower than their chest while you're looking at them from either the top or the side). Those characteristics don't have anything to do with how active your dog is, or how much (or little) you feed them. Exercise alone is not the most successful way to manage your dog's weight; there's a daily food quantity that will help your dog reach and maintain their healthy weight, regardless of their activity level.

When talking about food, Derek often runs into owners worrying that it doesn't seem like they're feeding their dogs enough food, or that their dog seems so active that it's impossible or unlikely for them to be considered medically overweight. Again, the big picture here is the objective appearance of your dog. If they meet the criteria for a healthy weight then they're a healthy weight.

Unfortunately, being overweight is correlated with a number of chronic illnesses that can shorten your dog's life-span. It can also make certain chronic illnesses, like arthritis, worse. No kidding, dogs as young as nine months can deal with arthritis. Their chonk is adorable, but it negatively impacts their experience of living.

I know this is gonna seem obvious, but it's got to be said. If your dog is overweight, the solution is feeding them less so that they eat less. And if your dog is underweight, the solution is getting them to eat more. Remember, that's how much your dog eats at mealtime in total over a twenty-four-hour period, not how often they eat it. Also, switching diets—even within the same brand!—may require changes in food volume, since each bite contains a different number of calories.

I know weight and body image can feel like a loaded conversation for so many reasons when discussing humans, but you can rest assured that the concept of an ideal weight for your pooch is all about keeping them in your life, healthy and feeling good, for as long as possible.

Water

If you're not thirsty after all that talk about food, I am, so let's pause for a water break. And a pee break, too, if your puppy is already home with you. Good? . . . Okay. Let's talk about that water.

Dogs are good at regulating their own water intake and drinking when they want or need to. It's your job as their human to make sure they have access to water whenever they need it. One major rule: make sure your dog drinks from the bowls inside, not the random puddles outside! Outside water, like lakes, rivers, and streams, can contain leptospirosis bacteria, which comes from wildlife urine. (So stagnant outdoor water bowls might fall under this category, too.) Lepto can make dogs supersick, and some dogs can even die from it. It's also zoonotic, which means it can be transferred from infected animals to humans via urine. When treating a dog who's sick with lepto, veterinarians have to use serious protective equipment and contamination strategies to avoid infection. Many infected patients die after extended, costly, miserable hospital stays. So it's a good rule of thumb to have no drinking water outside! Your pup is allowed to play in puddles, but no drinking from them. Bashi believes they're most fun if they have mud in them. Puddles, not bowls. This always leads to a bath, though, an outcome he rues.

Interestingly, dogs sweat less than humans do and sweat

isn't the primary way for them to thermoregulate. (That's just a fancy word for "control your own body temperature," whether you're a canine or a human.) Dog paw pads actually do sweat, though, just in case you were wondering. Dogs thermoregulate by panting. When panting, they rapidly inhale air and humidify it—that means they make the air moist, or a little bit wet—then exhale it. That action evaporates water from their nose and lungs and cools their body from the inside out. It's like they're carrying around their own air conditioners. Besides panting and having sweaty little paws, dogs also adjust their behavior. It's as easy as moving from sunshine to shade. Ultimately, it's your job to make sure your dog isn't stuck outside in the blazing sun without access to any shade or water. Their panting can't do all the work!

Snacks

Here's another major rule when it comes to dogs and food: dogs usually train humans more than humans train dogs. And the number one thing dogs use to train humans is food. An otherwise healthy dog doesn't "need" any snacks. **Need.** Ha. I suspect Rupert would argue that's a quaint way to talk about snacks, of all things. What kinda dog needs snacks? Like humans, they **require** snacks. They **must have** snacks. Snacks are what fuel their puppy dog eyes, keep their loyal hearts beating, ensure that they can cuddle to the best of their abilities. . . . And to that, Rupert, I say snacks are really not for puppies.[57] Even if he's just a tiny bit hungry in between meals.

---

57 "But what if it was for puppies?" You're welcome for this earworm: Matt Hobbs, "What If It WAS for Puppies? (Puppy Songs)," YouTube video, May 6, 2020, https://www.youtube.com /watch?v=N-39QOFChqc.

Friend, you must resist the puppy dog eyes. That adorable begging move is exactly how **you** end up trained and not your dog. It's your responsibility to make sure your puppy doesn't go overboard on the snacks, especially snacks made of people food. Munching away on snacks all day long can cause tummy aches and upset the delicate balance of maintaining a healthy body weight. Also, way more human food than you expect is toxic for your dog or might make them sick. (Grapes, onions, garlic—the list goes on. Google is your best friend here.[58])

I do carry around a little pouch to reward my pack when they do what I ask them to do during training or while out and about in the world. Most dogs are motivated enough by the simple things, so during training you can use the kibble your dog eats for their regular meals. (Make sure to balance these calories out with those from their regularly scheduled meals.) You don't actually have to pay for anything fancy to get your dog to do what you want. Though most dogs are also willing to be on very good behavior if it means they get to eat a McDonald's french fry. . . . Okay, okay. Half, only half. Just this once.

Tummy Problems

Some dogs do not have appetites that are satiated by something as simple as a french fry. I knew a dog named Charlie who loved to chew the fuzz off of tennis balls and swallow it, like cotton candy. Bashi enjoys tearing toys limb from limb and chomping on their stuffing. Rupert would (and has) ripped all the leaves off of houseplants and treated them like salad.

The nature of owning a dog means at some point they're

---

58   The Pet Poison Helpline (https://www.petpoisonhelpline.com/) is a useful resource here.

probably gonna eat something they shouldn't and you're gonna have to deal with the consequences. However, even if your pooch has managed to snack on something they shouldn't, it's probably gonna be okay.

For dogs, tummy upset usually looks like being off their food—not eating like they normally do, maybe—or having grumbly tummy noises. Any unusual GI upset should prompt at least a phone call to the vet (and sometimes a visit, depending on what's going on). There are some symptoms that definitely increase concern, though: diarrhea, vomiting, poor appetite, blood in your dog's poop, or bloody vomit. The superworrying symptoms are black, tarry stool—poop that's thick and sticky, because it usually means bleeding in their GI tract—and what looks like coffee grounds in their vomit (that means blood in their digestive system, because blood turns black when it's been digested).

If your dog full-on eats what the vet calls a foreign object, like, say, any of the above things mentioned,[59] or starts having any of those symptoms, you do have resources you can access. There's the ASPCA Animal Poison Control Center (the APCC),[60] which you can call twenty-four hours a day, every single day of the year. You'll pay a small fee to talk to animal poison control experts, but it's completely worth the peace of mind that comes from knowing how toxic a substance is and whether you need to follow up with a visit to the vet, either at the emergency room or the next day. The APCC are the people even Derek trusts with hard questions about when our pack eat things they shouldn't.[61]

---

59 Or nonfood items, or bones, as previously mentioned.

60 (888) 426-4435.

61 Yes, I called about the houseplant Rupert ate. Yes, the diarrhea was gnarly. No, I didn't have to bring him to see Derek.

If your dog does get into something toxic, sometimes the onset of symptoms can be delayed. Derek regularly deals with dogs who get into rat poison—unfortunately, one of the more common ways dogs are poisoned. There are several types of baits available on the market.[62] The baits tend toward fast-acting, lethal, and less treatable neurotoxins and renal toxins. If you think your dog has been poisoned, you need to go to the vet immediately. It's crucial to bring the package of the poison your dog got into—not a similar one, not one from the internet, *the* package. That way your vet will know what kind of poison your dog ingested and the appropriate treatment.[63] Scary, right? Our lives would be much easier if dogs wouldn't go sticking their noses in places they don't belong! Barring a perfectly behaved puppy (which is a misnomer along the same lines as a perfectly behaved toddler), the best call is for you to not keep stuff like rat poison in the house at all.

Aside from eating things like tennis ball fuzz or getting into toxic stuff, dogs can get something called pancreatitis, which is when their pancreas becomes inflamed. The pancreas is an organ that helps dogs (and people) digest food and produces hormones like insulin. Mostly, pancreatitis is caused by consuming really rich, fatty, oily foods (or rotten things, like trash and dead stuff). Symptoms can be as minor as being nauseated or as serious as causing damage to other organs. Even one teeny-tiny bite of something rich enough can trigger a flare-up in a sensitive dog. So it's smart to keep your dog away from

---

62 "Treating the Unknown Rodenticide in Pets," ASPCA Pro, https://www.aspcapro.org/resource/treating-unknown-rodenticide-pets.

63 If you're anxious and a little paranoid like me, symptoms of rat poison ingestion in a dog can include a bloody nose, bruising, and bloody urine.

pizza, fatty steak, and ice cream. (This is where we refer back up to them training you and note that you must stay strong! No giving in!)

You might have heard horror stories about bloat in dogs, too. Bloat is related to tummy aches in the same way that cutting off your finger is related to a paper cut, but the symptoms are useful to be able to identify. There are two different types of "bloat" to differentiate between: food bloat, which is seen fairly uncommonly by vets, and GDV (gastric dilatation-volvulus, sometimes called torsion). Food bloat is more accurately a severe episode of overeating; what happens when, say, a dog eats half a bag of dog food. Food bloat is uncomfortable but usually very manageable. However, it may mimic symptoms of GDV, and GDV is much more serious and dangerous.

GDV is one of the most severe, genuine surgical emergencies that your dog can experience. We don't know why GDV happens—veterinarians don't have a specific behavior to point out to prevent it. During GDV, the dog's stomach expands with gas (that's the dilatation part; "dilatation" means being stretched beyond the normal dimensions of the stomach). That expansion increases pressure inside the abdomen. In a GDV case, the dog's stomach also twists inside their abdomen. That combination of expansion and flipping causes major consequences, like blocking the blood supply from appropriate circulation, or stomach necrosis, where the stomach tissue dies. I'm not telling you this to try to terrify you; I swear. GDV tends to be very breed specific and overwhelmingly affects large- and giant-breed dogs. Symptoms include a tense, distended abdomen,[64] general weakness, pacing, retching

---

64 Families describe being able to literally watch their dog's stomach expand from the outside.

without producing vomit material, panting, or collapse. Those symptoms mimic other urgent medical problems, so this is hands down a trip to the vet, not a call to the APCC.

Big picture? Try hard to make sure your pup doesn't eat the fuzz off their tennis balls, dude. I can only suspect the mouthfeel is good, but it's good in kibble, too, okay? Don't even try to convince me you haven't tried it at least once. (Their kibble, not chewing on a tennis ball. I won't judge, either way.)

CHAPTER 4

Sleeping

Everyone says that cats are the best at napping (hence: "catnap"), but I am here to tell you that dogs give cats a run for their money when it comes to hitting the snooze button.[65] (Though the obvious solution here is to have a home full of both dogs and cats so they can all nap together. Or maybe that's just the solution our home has come up with.) On average, dogs sleep twelve to fourteen hours a day—and that number increases for puppies and senior dogs. There's not too much that's complicated about your fur friend catching a couple zzz's . . . except, of course, if you join them. Then you'll really learn how dang hard it is to get out of bed when you've got a dog cuddled up next to you. They exert some dog-specific gravity that pulls you back to the pillows, I swear. You've officially been warned. Do you have any idea how hard it was to get up to write this book as a direct result of an ensuing cuddle puddle?

Crate Training

Some of us get dogs because we don't have kids. Some of us have kids and a new dog is just a way to build our family even further. Either way, it doesn't take a rocket scientist to under-

---

65   Perhaps they're so good at it specifically because they don't *have* snooze buttons.

stand that a puppy is a lot like a baby: both spend tons of time sleeping because they're both spending tons of energy growing. Much like a baby, puppies also have an extremely accurate internal alarm clock. Rupert still wakes up at 7:00 am on the dot for breakfast, and there's no "please just let me doze for another five minutes" option when your dog is very! much! awake! for! food! (Sometimes this tendency abates as they get older; I occasionally have to wake old man Henry up by bringing his food to him in bed.)

As for where they sleep, I can pretty much guarantee that if your dogs see you on furniture (beds, couches, chairs) they will try to join you. Try lying on a dog bed before crawling into your own bed and you'll see exactly why that is—besides the pleasure of your company, a mattress is darn comfy. A dog pile lit by sunshine cuddled up with your favorite human is pretty much perfection, in your dog's brain. (Laundry still warm from the dryer is a close second, if Rupert had his say.) While all of these are perfectly acceptable, let me also introduce the idea of a crate.

Many humans balk at the concept, but crates are a good thing. Dogs are descended from wolves and crates are the evolved version of a den. They are warm, clean, the exact right size, and somewhere your dog will know they're safe. It's basically like giving your pup their own room.

What makes for a good crate? Aside from the whole clean and dry part (because they're inside your house!), they need to be big enough for your pup to stand up and turn around to get comfy before they lie down. Crates don't need much in the way of decoration, just something soft to lie on and maybe a comfort toy for some extra support—but only if your pup won't tear it apart while left to their own devices. If you're gone for a few hours, you might give your pup access to a water bowl inside the crate, but since dogs thermoregulate, it's not strictly necessary to do so. (We don't.)

The size of the crate is based on the size of the dog. You don't want a crate that's so big your dog can pee or poop in one corner and be far enough away from where they toileted to sleep in the opposite corner. Even at a young age, dogs are good about not soiling the space they're in—within reason! Young pups are more likely to have accidents in their crates than adult dogs until they're fully potty trained.

The most important thing, though, is that the crate should *never* be used as a tool for punishment. Crates aren't just stand-ins for dens; they're training tools. A dog in a crate is happy, content, and maybe napping. They're not eating furniture, peeing on the living room rug, or barking like a fool at the lizards[66] they can see through the front window by standing on the top of the couch—a stunt my Terrier mixes regularly pull and know they shouldn't.

Associating the crate with positivity means reliable use and enjoyment of said crate. That translates to freedom for you as an owner. Freedom to run errands, or focus on work, or just know your pup isn't getting into trouble (or making trouble!) while you're out of the house.

Crate training is something you'll have to build up to with your pup, but building up behaviors is the foundational building block of all dog training. First, bring the crate home even before your pup comes home for the first time. That way it starts as a normal part of the environment, something your dog can sniff and get used to. This is also why we feed our pack inside their crates—starting with the door open, at first. You can also

---

66   Or squirrels, or whatever animal exists for dogs to bark at in your climate.

give them high-value treats or toys inside the crate, so your dog can associate the crate with feelings of safety and contentment. (This is really a Jedi mind trick of the highest order.)

If you do all that setup right, your dog might not even notice when you close the door for the first time. If your pup does notice, though, make sure you open the door right away when they try to get out. Remember, we're trying to avoid all feelings of fear so there's not a link between "crate = scary." Then, like with all things, you just have to keep practicing. Eventually, you'll be able to close the door and your pup won't notice, won't mind, or both.

Once you have that down pat, you'll practice having your dog sit and stay politely before they're allowed to come out. It's also really important that if your dog is going into their crate for any amount of time when you won't be watching them, their collar **must** come off. This is a major safety issue; let's just say the horror stories about dogs strangulating themselves exist and are not fun to hear.

An adult dog can spend an extended period of time in their crate without issue once trained, all the way up to eight hours. Even puppies can safely hang out in a crate all night. Crying is going to be normal at first, but again, the more you link the crate with safety and positivity, the easier it'll be.

I still won't fault you if you want to take naps in bed with your doggo, though.

Sleeping in the Bed

I have no idea where the pesky rumor started that a dog sleeping in bed with you could be bad for you, but it's utter folly. Honestly, I'm starting to wonder if it started through the cat whisper network in an attempt to keep dogs away from all the squishy pillows and soft blankets. Exactly something a cat would do, eh?[67]

But, as with everything, there are exceptions to the rule. Unless the human in question has some kind of medical condition where limb compression from a lounging dog might cause injury (or a dog is dealing with something similar!), it should be okay. Your pup is not going to pass on some dog-specific parasite or disease to you just because you snuggle up with them for a good cuddle. Also, this is yet another good reason to make sure your dog is on monthly flea and tick preventative. Those nasties can hurt humans as well as dogs, so not having to worry about them means a safer snooze for everybody.

Lots of small dogs like to burrow under the covers. Rupert likes being beneath my legs as a calf rest; Bashi gets way too hot because of his long fur but isn't against sleeping beside me and using my shoulder as a chin pillow. As long as everybody is comfortable and there's enough room for all of us, dog-pile away! I will note that somehow the smallest dogs do manage to take up two-thirds of the entire bed.

You may need to change the bedsheets and do more laundry because you've invited your pup up with you, but that's just the name of the game: expect fur as a side effect of their love. I think it's worth it. Plus, it means warm laundry for your pup to take naps in, and clean sheets more often. Everyone wins.

If you want to offer your dog sleep options that aren't their crate or your bed, dog beds located around the house are always a solid choice. My pack is fortunate to live in a house where they're spoiled rotten. Crates, couches, human beds,

---

67 Our clowder of cats? Absolutely.

and dog beds: they nap where and when they want, and I either join them or take pictures of them because I think they're cute. Nesting is part of that wolf instinct buried deep in your dog's genetics. In most cases, flat beds are great, but some dogs like to burrow. They do make beds where dogs can nestle in or cover themselves up completely. Dog beds can be supercushy, with lots of padding, or simple as a yoga mat. Sometimes even just a rug is enough.

Dog beds are useful for naps. They're also sometimes useful for absolute and total destruction. . . . Even an old dog sometimes likes to give in to their base instincts once in a while and tear the bed to pieces! (No, I don't love it when any member of my pack decides to do this.) However, make sure your dog doesn't swallow what's inside the beds—that'll loop you back around to tummy problems and a possible visit to the vet real quick. (Eating the stuffing out of toys or beds can cause blockages in the dog's tummy or intestines.) Check the dog beds regularly to make sure your pup isn't chowing down on seams they shouldn't. Also, just like with bedsheets, throw their bedding into the wash regularly to make sure it smells good, for everybody's sake.

Having beds around the house is especially important for giant breeds, like Great Danes. It's important for arthritic pets like Henry, too—his sore bones need somewhere soft to land. Our whole house is tiled, and hard floors can sometimes feel good for a short period of time (like when it's hot outside! Cool tile is fabulous for thermoregulation), but having lots of opportunities to be able to lie down on something comfortable is a necessity. Can you imagine a human having no furniture for themselves in their own homes? It would be like that. Long story short, provide your pup places to nap where they can be comfy and have sweet dreams when they do.

Sleep Schedules

All dogs run on their own schedule, the same way people do. Dogs have a natural circadian rhythm; Rupert's happens to be set for early to bed, early to rise. He's lucky I think he's cute; otherwise I wouldn't put up with getting him breakfast that early, lemme tell ya.

Of course, just like with all things, dogs train their humans when it comes to sleeping. Derek sums it up succinctly: "Don't train them into habits you don't want them to keep." If only I could tell them that! Anyways, all that means is that if your dog wants to go out to pee six times overnight you probably shouldn't acquiesce to every request, because then your dog would know they could get away with it. (As usual, old dogs and dogs with health issues are excluded. Getting older sometimes makes it so dogs have to potty more frequently, and various health issues—or the medications dogs have to take to deal with those health issues—might also make your dog get up more frequently.)

Of course, Rupert being up early doesn't offset his naps—even as he gets older. Not all dogs sleep eight hours straight through. (Heck, not all humans sleep eight hours straight through, but that's a whole separate book.) Some humans find themselves concerned that their dogs get up in the night, but have you never gotten up for water, or because you had a weird dream, or because you heard something? Dogs are as individual as people. Rupert likes to be in bed long before midnight; Bashi prefers a good sleep-in after staying up late with me, plus a lazy midmorning breakfast.

As far as that whole dreaming thing, that's gonna depend on the dog, too. Rupert dreams heavily and hard—he kicks with his back legs and even howls. It scared the hell out of me the first time he did it in the middle of the night. He was passed out on my chest, so I woke up from a dead sleep and in my haze I thought he was having a seizure. Nope. Just a really good dream about chasing something. Bashi has a tendency to snore like a freight train. Seriously, though, all of this is normal. (I mean, as long as none of us think too hard about the fact that we just power down our brains for big chunks of time and have major hallucinations in our imagination while sound asleep. Because that's really flippin' weird. And . . . also a totally separate book.)

Sleep Issues

Sleep is weird, and most of the things that happen during it are normal. There are a few "just in case" things to look out for, though. First, keep an eye out for when a sleeping dog (and especially a young pup) has breathing issues in their sleep or can't be easily roused when they're crashed out. I don't mean when they're conked out and stuck in a good dream—I mean when it's nearly impossible to get them up, awake, and acting normal. Those are good signs for a trip to the vet. You'll become very accustomed to your dog's schedule, the same way they do with ours, so you'll know if something seems "off," like if your dog is sleeping more or less than their normal schedule. If it's bothering you, a chat with the vet is never a bad idea. Generally speaking, the vet has more knowledge in their head about dogs than most people will ever know, so it's worth the time, effort, and money to ask them, if only for the peace of mind. Derek works for a practice where every phone call gets directed to a veterinarian, free of charge, before you even come in, so he can tell clients whether it's worth a trip or not. So call. Seriously.

My Terriers have long muzzles, but dogs with squished faces (like French Bulldogs, Boston Terriers, or Pugs) are more likely to deal with sleep issues because of their breeding. Dogs with squished faces are described as "brachycephalic." Since they have short noses, long soft palates (the soft part on the roof of the mouth), and narrow nares (a fancy word for "nostrils"), they'll make even more noise in their sleep than Bashi does. They snuffle and snorfle and sniffle. It's nearly impossible to take a nap next to one of them, speaking from personal experience. It's like trying to nap with a human who has sleep apnea but doesn't use a fancy machine to help with their breathing (because it *is* sleep apnea, just sleep apnea for dogs).[68] Same rules apply: if a brachycephalic dog snores a lot or seems like they stopped breathing in their sleep for prolonged periods of time, chat with the vet about how to help.

Some brachycephalic dogs end up having to have surgery to help them breathe better. Their vet might suggest surgically changing the shape of their soft palate, widening their nostrils, or even removing something called the everted laryngeal saccules, little sacs that live in the trachea (where dogs breathe). These sacs can cause obstruction by being too floppy and blocking the airway. It sort of sounds like cosmetic surgery for dogs, but the kind that's necessary because we all have to breathe, especially when we sleep. Not being able to breathe is not just terrifying but exhausting. You can't get rest if you're waking up, unable to inhale or exhale. This isn't just an issue

---

68 Similar to sleep apnea for dogs being plain ol' sleep apnea, Derek gets the question, "Is there such a thing as doggy Xanax?" a lot. The answer? Yeah, Xanax. A lot of conditions and medications that humans experience and take overlap with what canines can deal with, too.

while sleeping, either; ultimately, the way humans have bred brachycephalic features into dogs isn't cute. It's a problematic trait that punishes and kills our pets because we want them to be aesthetic. But ask me how I really feel.

That covers the big stuff for sleeping. I'd never presume to tell you what to do, but now might be a good time to go grab a nap with your pooch. Sweet dreams!

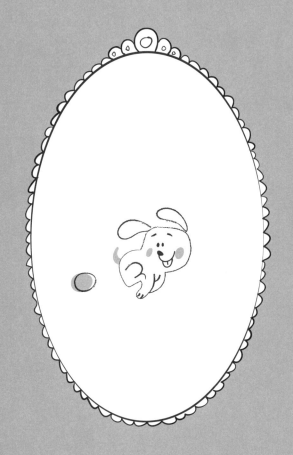

CHAPTER 5

Playing

Puppies love to play. Most dogs, actually, really enjoy playing in one form or another. There are all kinds of fancy toys available on the market and you can spend a pretty penny to placate your pup, but the vast majority of dogs will literally play with trash straight out of the garbage if it means you'll just spend time with them.

Luckily, playing fulfills a bunch of important needs. Play sessions help your dog learn motor skills, like rolling, pouncing, and shaking. Playing with other dogs teaches your dog how to communicate (to speak dog, as it were). Playing also burns off energy, helps to teach and enforce certain behaviors, and keeps their brain stimulated and busy (which eventually makes them tired!). Dogs who don't get to spend enough time playing will often turn to destructive behaviors to entertain themselves and get rid of that excess energy. Don't underestimate how important play is for your pup—and especially don't get a puppy unless you're committed to spending a good amount of time focused specifically on play.

Toys

There are literally so many dog toys offered on the market that if I started counting now I'd keep going until I kicked the bucket. There's always some newfangled dog-related invention. Don't get me wrong; plenty of those toys are great. I've tried a good number of 'em, trust me. But here's the thing about dogs: they're just as happy playing tug-of-war with your dirty undies stolen straight out of the laundry basket as they are playing with whatever is the latest fad.[69]

Now some dogs do pick favorite toys. Roland had a favorite toy until he crossed the Rainbow Bridge at age thirteen.[70] It was his baby until the end. But by the time we adopted Bashi, he was almost a year old and had been living on the streets for most of that time. It was too hardscrabble for him to have a toy to carry around all the time. Rupert has a cute little purple duck he alternately cuddles and tries to kill. Ezra has never quite gotten the hang of toys (I'm not sure he's ever had one before our house), and Henry could give two hecks about toys. Having a comfort toy is totally normal and okay, so long as said toy is in good condition.

Our house has a whole box full of toys in the middle of the living room. The pack is allowed to play with any of these toys anytime they want. I specifically try to buy toys made of tough materials, like durable fabric, rope, or rubber. My pack may be small, but they are all unquestionably mighty, and will tear most soft toys to shreds. (How many times can you say the word "toy" before it stops looking like a real word?)

Because my pack is prone to destruction, I check the toy box regularly to make sure nobody has pulled out squeakers, or eaten ribbons, buttons, or strings. I am of the mind that toys

---

69　Don't let them do this. This is a recipe for a blockage and a very expensive trip to the vet.

70　Yes, this euphemism means "when your dog dies, whether naturally or by euthanasia."

with pieces that can come off somewhat easily don't make for safe toys. I have also been a dog parent for long enough to know that they are remarkably adept at removing pieces that weren't necessarily designed to be removed, so I always monitor them when giving them new toys, just to make sure no major messes or trouble ensues.

The same goes for making sure toys are the right size for my dogs. Smaller dogs benefit from smaller toys; Rupert literally can't fit a "normal"-sized tennis ball in his mouth, unlike the golden retrievers next door. It's a fine line to determine appropriate sizing for toys, but generally you don't want a toy to be so small they can choke or so big they might hurt themselves.

Another place to pay attention is to your dog's teeth. Lots of things sold at the pet store aren't actually great for your dog. Capitalism isn't looking out for the little pup, that's for sure. I know you've seen bones and hooves at the store. They might smell good to your doggo, but they're a bad idea. They're so physically hard your dog could easily break their teeth on them, or ingest big pieces that stop their insides up like a cork.[71] Derek has even treated dogs who've gotten round bones stuck around their jaw, which then required surgical removal. No, thank you—to the pain *and* the ensuing veterinary bill! Rawhide and pig's ears are off the list, too—your dog can chew them into pulp that they can choke on, or again . . . Yup. Blockage. I know. Booooring, but this is real life. When I was nineteen and Roland was my first dog as an "adult," I didn't know any better and gave him a rawhide stick. He choked on

---

71   I don't know how many times I can tell you "obstruction means surgery," but count this as another.

it, and I had to fish it out of his throat with my pinky. It was terrifying and I wouldn't want any being—dog or human—to go through the same experience.[72]

If the dog you get is a puppy, they're going to have an insatiable desire to put things in their mouth and chew. Some dogs don't actually grow out of that, actually. Fortunately, there are plenty of treats at the store made specifically to be consumed and to focus on mouth health. (Greenies, as mentioned, are a great example.)

Occasionally, I'll grab a bunch of the inexpensive stuffies from the pet store and dump the whole plethora of toys on the floor just so I can watch the pack go totally bonkers, barking and generally causing chaos and bedlam. It's great for everybody, but *especially* the dogs.

Usually, I'll rotate their toys out regularly. This ensures they don't get bored with the ones they have. Sometimes I hide the toys around the house so the pack will find them. (Behind pillows, under the bed, in corners.) Sneaky, but it works. Toys that keep their brains busy in different ways are good, too. Rupert's purple duck baby is good for gnawing on; we've got some tennis balls for rolling; there's one long toy that's great for carrying; there's a chunky one for digging into and shaking. Lots of options to keep the pack busy!

Of course, it's not just the toys that are important; it's what we do with the toys. Interactive play is necessary for blowing

---

72   Just like humans, dogs have an epiglottis. It's a hard cartilage structure that lies over the windpipe at the back of the throat and works as a shield to direct food toward the stomach instead of down the airway. If you have to perform an oral sweep, you may feel the dog's epiglottis and accidentally confuse it for a bone or other foreign object. Doesn't mean the oral sweep isn't helpful, just means bodies are weird, man.

off steam and reducing boredom and stress. So here are some games you can play with your pooch!

Fetch

Whenever I try to get Ezra to play fetch with me by throwing a ball, he turns around and looks at me like, *Hellooooo, this is not my problem; you're the one who threw the thing, you go get it*. Eventually—well, sometimes—he humors me enough to at least run after it, but he rarely returns. I am perpetually trying to make fetch happen.[73] Mostly I suspect he finds it funny to watch me gesture at the ball until he finally does come back, sans.

The game of fetch—you throw a thing, your dog retrieves the thing and brings it back, you throw it again—is obsessively fun for some dogs. Bashi would fetch forever if he could. There are ways to teach dogs to play fetch, if you're serious about training. I am neither skilled enough to try to teach you through the pages of this book nor certified as a trainer, but it can be done. Trust me enough to know that fetch exists. Some dogs understand it instinctively, some dogs require training to get it, and some dogs will never understand or even bother to care.

Tug-of-War

Tug-of-war is the Sisyphean task of pulling hard on a toy but not actually getting anywhere, much like trying to pay off your student loans or buy a house in this economy. This game, however, unlike those exhausting trials of existing in the

---

73   Thank you to the millennials who laughed at this joke.

twenty-first century, is a great way for your dog to exercise their predatory nature safely. It does require rules. First, you gotta have a release command. In our house, we use "drop it." Whenever a human says "drop it," the dog or dogs in question are supposed to let go of whatever is in their mouths, no questions asked. Sometimes we use this command when we aren't even playing, to get potentially dangerous things out of their mouth that our dog might not know they shouldn't be chewing on. Having a release command is a deeply important skill for your dog to have.

Once your dog masters "drop it," you'll get to play tug-of-war. (Again, I am not skilled enough to teach you "drop it" via this book. I implore you to spend the money on training classes or hiring a private trainer. TikTok and YouTube are rife with dog-training videos and instructions, but please do your research before settling on one of these trainers. Avoid trainers who use pain, fear, or dominance as part of their training routine. Most importantly, consistency is key.)

Even with little dogs, tug-of-war requires a decent amount of space, usually without distractions or clutter you might trip over while playing. This game, often more than others, might cause your dog to growl. I'll talk more about body language and speaking dog in a later chapter, but growling is simply a form of speaking dog. You should absolutely not train your dog out of growling. After all, generally speaking, a growl is simply a sound a dog makes. Some dogs growl to let those around them know they're feeling nervous. Some dogs growl while playing because they're giving in to their wolfish ancestry. A growl unto itself isn't a bad thing and teaching a pup that they can't growl might mean humans miss important communication. A dog who's taught they're not allowed to growl might go straight to biting . . . but again, that's in a later chapter.

Anyways, growling while playing isn't necessarily a bad thing, especially if your dog is in a play bow and their tail is wagging, but when a growl happens it usually means we take a little break and bring things down to a calmer level.

Ditto on hitting the pause button if your dog's teeth accidentally make contact with you (or another dog!) while playing. That's a big no-no. Whenever there is teeth-on-skin contact in our house, we make a high-pitched yelping noise and follow up with the "drop it" command.

Then we take the toy and walk away for half a minute or so. This lets your pup know that they've gotten too intense and they need to bring it down a notch. The yelping sounds like playing with another puppy and helps them remember they need to be gentle. Stepping away is a nonviolent way to communicate that biting causes your dog to lose your attention, which they desperately want.

Also, a good thing to remember while playing games with your pup is that letting them win is a great way to build up their confidence. I won't fault you if you insist on a tug-of-war championship with included trophy, though. Just don't be surprised if your dog lets you win cuz they feel bad for you.

Chase

Chase is my household's favorite game, but we absolutely do not play it indoors. Chase in our house is so rough-and-tumble it may or may not have led to knocked-over food, drinks, and maybe even furniture. Learn from my mistakes.

Dogs love to chase. Each other, their tails, or just for the sheer joy of running. There aren't rules; there's just chase. Okay, I mean, I guess there technically are rules, but not for the chasing part. That's basic. See your friend, follow your friend at full speed, repeat. Chasing is a natural canine instinct, and there's nothing more perfect than doing laps around the back-yard running after each other—or a toy. Whatever, most dogs aren't picky.

Of course, our backyard has a big, tall fence, one that my dogs are way too short to jump over. That's not true for all dogs; I've met more than one Lab at the dog park who thought a fence was just an invitation to pretend they were an Olympic hurdler, but I digress.

The biggest trick of chase is making sure your dog doesn't chase after cars, cats, birds, squirrels, or anything else that might make for a recipe for disaster. Similarly, it's important that they don't attack if they catch something—following the prohibition on biting I discussed earlier. The difficulty in re-sisting the impulse varies by breed,[74] which is part of why dogs should always have their collars and leashes on while outside. It's rude to chase other animals and cars can kill your dog dead.

Much like having a "drop it" command, I strongly urge you to train your dog to have a fail-safe stop command. This command is one where they know you mean business, no BS, no kidding around. In our house, this command is "STOP." It is said in a voice that terrifies everyone who hears it.[75] Dogs know this command means to stop where they are, sit, and turn around to make eye contact with their humans. Again, I am not the right expert to guide you through that process in this book, but please hire a trainer or use the internet to teach a "STOP" command to your dog. It could save their life.

---

74   Try reining in a greyhound. I dare you.
75   This is a cousin to the Mom voice.

Catch

Rupert is the kind of dog who thinks chasing is fine but prefers games with some kind of payoff at the end. I suspect it's because he's a Rat Terrier—bred specifically for catching rodents, which means his brain wants to grab and shake. It's rather impressive to watch him throw his entire body into the process of catching, though sometimes I'm terrified he's going to go hurtling off the edge of the bed or the couch. I've spent most of his life catching *him* from falling, so I'm not sure he believes gravity exists.

Rupert loves to catch toys thrown at him but doesn't have the paw-eye coordination to grab a moving treat out of the air. You may want to experiment with your dog to see what works best—treats, toys, and balls are all options. There are even assistive devices to help you throw the ball farther than you'd be able to otherwise! (I admit I've even been eyeing a machine that you can teach your dog to load the ball into so it will auto-throw a ball and keep them entertained without your involvement, but that requires an investment of cash I haven't quite been willing to make—yet.)

Dog Park

Once you figure out the basics of playing with your pooch, you might start to wonder about where you can go to play without being stuck at home. Enter: the dog park. Dog parks are places humans have created specifically for dogs to go play together out in public. Dog parks can be all shapes and sizes, from a small patch of grass in an apartment complex to a square of Astroturf in a big city to actual gigantic miles of open space with lakes or even an ocean to splash around in. The world outside the safety of your home is so big, it will blow your dog's mind.

Of course, the dog park comes with two major liabilities: other dogs and their people. Unfortunately, the reality is that not all dogs have the same level of training and manners—and neither do their humans. When you venture out in public, you take big risks. You don't know if you're going to be interacting with dogs who have been socialized to be around other dogs, and not everybody is friendly when they meet a stranger—pooch or person. Once, Roland and I were out at a park we'd gone to regularly for years. We came face-to-face with this big dog. He started wagging his tail, big ol' grin on his face, normal dog communication for "friendly" and "let's play." Roland went up to say hi and *boom*, that other dog went after him, all teeth and fury. Scared me half to death. Roland was okay, but we had to go to the vet for X-rays to make sure. Also, the phone number the owner gave me for follow-up was a fake one. Jerk.

Ultimately, any opportunity for physical contact between dogs is a potential opportunity for some kind of physical altercation. Any pet will bite some being—dog or human—under the right circumstances. I mean, dogs **are** tiny versions of wolves. We haven't magically domesticated them into being people—there's still wild animal in them.[76] I'm not saying your dog is going to be the rude one at the dog park; I'm just saying it can happen.

The altercation with Roland is part of why keeping a leash on your dog is so important. Even if it's an off-leash park, the leash dragging on the ground gives you something to grab on to if anything goes funky. (Of course, your dog should never be

---

76 Heck, I've certainly been angry enough to want to nip at someone. I'm positive I've growled in anger before, and I'm not a canine.

out of your sight, so their leash won't get caught on anything that might make it hard for them to breathe.) Again, this is another situation where the "STOP" command is imperative.

If a fight does happen, you as a human aren't supposed to get in between the dogs. It rarely helps mitigate the situation, but it almost certainly puts yourself at a potentially life-altering risk. I won't lie, though—I jumped right in and grabbed Roland. Adrenaline makes you do things you rationally know you probably shouldn't, and my gut instinct was to protect my much smaller dog. I'm very fortunate no one got hurt, myself included. If you really have to try to break up a dogfight and there's no leash to pull on, you can pull from their back legs to avoid getting your hands in the danger zone. Dogs will usually turn their full attention on attacking the person or people trying to break up the fight. Unfortunately, it's better to just let the fight play out the way it's going to, even though that's terrifying, awful, and potentially leads to injuries or death. I'm sorry, I don't mean to scare you. This is, however, a good moment to remind you that a dog who sits or returns to their owner on command isn't chasing another dog (or getting farther away from you!). And a dog who's paying attention to the training treats in your little hip bag is going to be too busy to get up in another dog's face.

It's not just about manners, either. You don't know if other dogs have had all their vaccinations, which means you could be exposing your dog to all kinds of infectious diseases. And Dog knows we've met some very rude humans while out at parks, too.

So yes, dog parks can be a really good way for your dog to socialize, meet other dogs, and get used to being around people in a new environment. No question, running in a wide-open field can be a joy for your doggo. But nowadays we do most of our playing at home instead. My pack is too precious for me to take risks with.

Swimming

If dog parks aren't your jam, water might be the place for you and your dog. As with pretty much everything, your dog's preferences are going to vary. Not every pooch enjoys a splish-splash, but those who do provide us with as much entertainment as we give them! Salt water, chlorinated water, plain ol' rainwater—it doesn't make a difference so long as your pup gets a good rinse after the fact. Actually, make sure they don't hop into any pools immediately after the pool has had chemicals put in. They don't always close their eyes properly, there's delicate pink skin beneath that fur, and they can't seal their mouth and nose as easily as we humans can. That means potential exposure to pool chemicals before they disperse to safe levels. Also, even dogs who have spent their whole lives swimming may end up with what's called aspiration pneumonia, which is where water or other material (like vomit) is inhaled into their lungs instead of swallowed properly. This can cause inflammation and can lead to infection.[77] Signs of aspiration pneumonia are coughing, especially a cough with a heavy rattling sound or a cough that causes vomiting, and breathing difficulty in general. These signs usually set in within an hour or two of the event—usually when they're biting, chewing, or snapping at water and inhaling it at the same time; if waves hit them; if they're playing hard in water and breathing heavily; or if they get dunked under.

The big thing to worry about when it comes to water is making sure your dog can actually stay afloat. No, dogs aren't

---

77   Remember the epiglottis? That's designed to help stop exactly this.

all born with an innate swimming skill. Assuming a dog can swim right off the bat is like assuming a toddler can. Important to note that *they can't*. Just like kids, dogs need to be eased into swimming, with little introductions, lots of praise, and maybe a treat or two.

Flotation devices are superimportant, too. Especially if you're going to be out on a boat or near an ocean or lake. Tides can easily sweep little dogs away. The best kind of dog personal flotation device has a chin rest to help support their head and keep their nose above water, plus handles that can be easily grabbed in case of an emergency. You'll need to make sure it fits them perfectly—make sure it isn't too big or too small—and focus on high-visibility colors like bright yellow, which helps with safety. Most aren't expensive, but worth every penny for investing in safety.

The cleanliness of the water your pup is swimming in is really important. Stagnant water that's standing instead of flowing can contain toxic or infectious elements. If your pup does get into stagnant water, be on alert for symptoms of lepto and giardia. With lepto, you want to keep an eye out for fever, reluctance to move, a stiff gait, shivering, and not wanting to eat. Giardia symptoms include diarrhea, gas, tummy hurting, vomiting. Yes, giardia gets passed along in water, too. Giardia and lepto can both be treated with meds, but they have to be treated early and aggressively. Trust me, it's better to just not put your dog in the situation to begin with.

The other big thing to look out for when it comes to water and dogs is blue-green algae. Confusingly, it's not actually always blue-green in color; sometimes it's red or brown colored. It occurs in freshwater or salt water, or even in pools or decorative ponds if they're not regularly cleaned. The "algae" is actually a cyanotoxin, which can cause respiratory or liver failure if ingested. Symptoms for blue-green algae poisoning depend on the type of toxin ingested, and can range from liver damage (vomiting, diarrhea, weakness, pale gums, and black, tarry stool) to neurotoxicity (excessive salivation, muscle tremors or rigidity, blue gums, and difficulty breathing). Unfortunately, blue-green algae poisoning can set in within moments and there's not a lot of treatment options. The prognosis is almost always fatal. Pay attention for news stories about algae blooms in your area.

After swimming in any water, your dog will need a good body rinse and to have their ears cleaned out with a dog-safe ear wash that has ascetic acid in it, to help dry the ears out. Getting your pup's ears good and dry is important, but making sure there's no sand or seashells inside is important, too.

Those are the big rules for playing in water. I hope you'll find a dog who loves water as much as you do. I've never managed that feat, but maybe one day I'll luck into a merdog to play in the ocean with me. . . .

CHAPTER 6

Health

The First Eight Weeks

Usually, you'll bring a puppy home when they're about eight or nine weeks old, though that might change depending on the breed of puppy. (Toy breeds, the kind of dogs that are teeny-tiny itty-bitty, might not come home until they're a little bit older because they can be so delicate.) Generally speaking, though, it's important for puppies to stay with their mom and littermates for the full eight or nine weeks because they have to grow up.

Lots of important things happen for the first eight weeks of a puppy's life. Puppies are pretty helpless at the beginning, just like human babies are. Their eyes don't even open until they're almost two weeks old. Also, puppies are born deaf. They don't develop hearing until they're almost three weeks old. Of course, puppies rely on mom for food by nursing from her—they start weaning off her milk at around four weeks old, but some puppies don't stop nursing entirely until they're about eight weeks old.

For the first eight weeks of your pup's life, their mom also helps teach them how to get along with other dogs. Since my dogs are street dog rescues, I don't know if any of them had siblings, but normally dogs' parents and siblings teach them to play and share things like toys and food. Puppies also develop a lot of their personality during the first few weeks of their existence.

Depending on how your dog comes into your life, you may not know their exact age. This is true for my current pack; I don't know when any of them were born. Roland was bought from a family who owned his mom, so I knew how old he was and could celebrate his actual birthday. For everybody else, we celebrate their adoption date as their birthday. Sometimes people will refer to this as their dog's "Gotcha!" day.

However, even without knowing the day they came into the world, we can make a very rough guesstimate of a dog's age using their teeth. Puppies have puppy teeth (which are very sharp!). Those pointy little suckers eventually fall out. Most dogs either swallow their baby teeth or lose them while playing, so it's rare to find baby teeth. Then dogs have adult teeth that come into their mouth from approximately four to six months of age. Being able to guess a dog's age from their teeth isn't an exact science. Some breeds have a propensity for worse dental issues than others, and some dogs (especially rescues!) didn't have access to the dentist through their lives. That means they may be missing teeth or have dental disease that makes their mouth look "older" than they actually are.

Some dogs, like Rupert, have what I jokingly call shark mouth, or double canines. This just means his grown-up teeth came in, but his baby teeth didn't fall out. This most commonly happens with canine teeth, because they have the longest tooth roots (the actual body of the tooth inside the jaw), which anchor the tooth into the jawbone and makes it less likely to fall out. We had Rupert's extras pulled when he was a little bit older and put under anesthesia to be neutered.

Dogs who are taken from their litter before eight or nine weeks will often have socialization issues, like anxiety or higher levels of stress. If possible, you want to give your pup as long as you can with their mom and their littermates to help them develop positively and succeed later in life.

Regular Veterinary Checkups

I've talked a lot about the vet, this mysterious entity you apparently have to bring your dog to regularly, who eats up all your money and who scares all the dogs. Let's start out with the most important part of this conversation: your veterinarian is a friend, not a foe. They're looking out for your dog's best interests, which is usually in your best interest as your dog's family. Like the human doctor, visiting a vet can be scary, especially if your dog doesn't feel good. The vet's office probably smells like fear to your poor pooch. But I promise you, crossing all my fingers and toes and even my eyes, that visiting the vet is so, so important there are hardly enough words to describe how much you have to go.

As you probably already know, the vet is a doctor who specializes in medicine for pets. Vets go to school for years and years[78] so they know how to take care of all kinds of things that happen to dogs and cats and other animals that humans keep in their houses.[79] Typically, you bring your pooch to their office, which is sometimes called a practice, a hospital,

---

78   The same amount of time as human doctors. Four years of college, four years of vet school, and sometimes two to four years of specialty education after that.

79   Vets also learn about farm animals and sometimes even exotic animals while at vet school; Derek has some choice stories about being up to his elbow in cow from the back end that are worth hearing over a cocktail.

or a clinic.[80] The vet certainly takes appointments for when your dog isn't feeling good, but it's superextra-very important that puppies *especially* go to the vet for a checkup after they come home for the first time. This first appointment will focus on preventative care, which means taking care of your dog's health long before you have an acute problem show up.

Of course, regular checkups are a necessary part of being a puppy. That first visit is just the start: you're going to go every three to four weeks until they're roughly four months old because you have to get their puppy vaccinations out of the way. Once the rounds of vaccinations are complete, your next visit will usually focus on having your pet neutered. I promise to answer those questions in a separate, specific section later in this chapter.

Once your dog ages out of puppyhood, you won't see the vet as frequently. Well, kinda. From the time your dog is one until they're seven, you should schedule them for at least an annual checkup. Once they hit seven, your dog is considered geriatric, the fancy word for old. After officially becoming an old doggo, your pup should go for bi-annual exams—that means twice a year—because getting older usually means bodies act up more frequently. Those bi-annual exams then happen until a dog crosses the Rainbow Bridge. I know, that seems like practically forever from now, but every dog has their day. (That part never stops sucking, no matter how many times you go through it.)

Basically, though, seeing the vet more frequently is always a better call than not. After all, the best-case scenario is you have a happy checkup and the vet doesn't find anything, right?

---

80   This seems to be a local vernacular choice. Californian Derek hates when Floridian Ace calls it a vet clinic.

Next best-case option is the vet finds something early and it requires only mild intervention instead of a catastrophic illness diagnosis. Preventative care is worth a pound of cure, or something like that. I don't think you can measure either of those things on a scale, but it sounds good when you say it out loud.

There's an organization called the American Animal Hospital Association (AAHA! Ha. Ha-ha. It sounds like I'm laughing. Ha-ha. Aa-ha.), which has been around for ninety years, that helps vet practices and pet owners keep track of all the different things pets need throughout their lives. There's a bunch of resources on their website that you can check out regularly to make sure you're on top of everything your pup needs for their life stage.[81] You can even print out checklists and put them on the fridge to make sure nothing gets forgotten.

As for what a trip to the vet looks like: depending on where you live, you'll either drive, walk, wheel, or commute to your vet's hospital. You want to make an appointment first; some practices let you do this online, but making a phone call is tried and true, too. When you get there with your pet, you'll usually check in and wait for a little bit either in the car or in a waiting room before they call you back. Some emergency hospitals give you the option to be back in the treatment area with your pet, but that's more unusual than not. You'll want to make sure your dog is collared and on a leash. If they're small (or anxious, especially around other pets), having them in a crate isn't a bad idea.

Once called back to a private exam room, you'll probably meet a technician or a nurse first. They'll check in with you, take some health history, and go over basic info to make sure they've got what they need (like why you're there for the visit).

---

81   "Resource Center," AAHA, https://www.aaha.org/aaha-guidelines /life-stage-canine-2019/resource-center/.

After that, you hopefully won't have to wait too long before you meet the vet![82]

The vet is usually really lovely, and you can tell they just want to take care of your baby. A good vet will come down to your pet's level and meet them first, say hi, and give them some scratches to make them feel safe.[83] There's almost always a big table with a counter that sometimes they lift your dog up onto, but just as often the vet will come down on the floor. Those tables can be really scary for dogs, who don't usually spend a lot of time up that high.

Once they've been properly introduced (though no butt sniffing; introduced by human standards only), the vet will perform a physical exam. That means they'll do a nose-to-tail evaluation, checking out your dog's anatomy and looking for any abnormalities that might indicate your dog is sick. Really good vets are sometimes so subtle while doing a physical exam that it looks like they're just petting your dog. Seriously, it's slick. In reality, they're looking at your dog's eyes, their teeth, feeling their belly, listening to their heart—all of the little details they pick up on will help them rule out tons of diseases and make sure your dog is doing their best. Usually while the vet is checking your dog out, they'll ask you questions about what's going on with them. Big questions will revolve around if anything has changed lately, like your dog's behavior or what they've been eating or other important details like that. Derek swears that combo of conversation with owner and physical exam of dog performed regularly is a powerful way to learn about your dog's health.

---

82   If there is a wait, it's almost always because your vet had to deal with a serious emergency. Please be kind to your veterinary staff.

83   Unless your dog demonstrates that they're not into it!

Depending on what's going on, an exam can also include having blood drawn and bloodwork performed. Bloodwork can help the vet evaluate the status of your dog's organs, like their liver or kidneys; check their blood sugar; or even figure out specifics about their immune system or blood, like their red blood cell, white blood cell, or platelet count. Sometimes the vet might also order what's called a fecal test, where they take a sample of your dog's poop to test for parasites (or to perform more specific tests depending on breed, lifestyle, age, or certain medical conditions). When your dog gets older, regular checkups might involve X-rays, eye pressure testing, or thyroid testing. A good vet will cater the physical exam to what's going on with the dog's body as a result of their age and life experience. Other than that, a lot of regular visits involve vaccinations, which I'll talk about soon. I promise.

While introductions don't involve sniffing butts, I'm sorry to be the one to tell you that the vet will take your dog's temperature by putting a thermometer up their bum. It's the most accurate way to get the information. A good vet will make sure they use lots of lubrication, though, and usually it's very quick, I swear! Bashi still flinches, even after all these years. It never really stops being surprising. The joys of being a dog, huh?

On the bright side, vets almost always give your pup a treat when done. So at least there's that. Once you and your vet finish the exam and talk through whatever needs to happen next, you'll either take home medications or have them called in to your local pharmacy for pickup. Please feel free to ask any and all questions you can think of here. A good vet either will have answers for you or will find out what they don't know, because they truly can't know everything. If your vet makes you feel uncomfortable or afraid to ask questions, it's worth it to find a different vet—for your sake and your dog's.

After the appointment concludes, you'll head back out to the waiting room where the front desk will collect payment and schedule any needed follow-ups. In a lot of ways, it's very similar to seeing a human doctor.

Emergency Vets and Specialists

If you're very lucky, you will go through the entire life of your dog without having to go to the emergency vet or see any specialists. Unfortunately, this kind of medicine exists for a reason: because we often need them, even if we really don't *want* to need them.

As I said earlier, the whole goal of regular checkups at the vet is to avoid seeing the emergency vet or any kind of veterinary specialists, but sometimes life happens. The emergency vet is a kind of specialist who provides medical care to animals, just like the regular vet in terms of credentials. The big difference is that the emergency vet usually practices medicine for emergency situations or medical issues that happen outside of normal business hours. That means if there's an accident, like your pup eats too much chocolate or gets into something they shouldn't or accidentally breaks a bone, you bring them to the emergency vet, the same way people visit the doctor at the emergency room. Usually, the emergency vet is open twenty-four hours a day, seven days a week, because accidents have a tendency to happen at the most inopportune moments.

Specialists will vary based on what kind of medicine they specialize in. Just like with humans, there are specialists for specific diseases. This includes, but isn't limited to, specialists like oncologists, for cancer; surgical specialists; and even veterinary behaviorists, who specialize in behavior. Specialists will usually have additional years of education beyond vet school, and likely have completed internships or other requirements to be categorized as specialists. Your regular vet will most likely be able to direct you toward their preferred specialist in whatever category you might need.

Derek and I have had a lot of pets over the years, and one of the things we do to make sure we know what to do in an emergency situation is figure out who our local emergency vet is ahead of time. That means we have the information on hand before we're in a panic, worried about one of the pack, and potentially stressing about all the things we need to do to manage an emergency. Before anything goes down medically, we visit the emergency practice, meet the vet there, and take a tour. We put the number to the emergency vet on the fridge and in our phones. We make sure to have the address in our phones, too, so we can just type it into the map app and go, go, go! If we go on vacation and someone else stays behind to watch the pack, we always make sure to include the emergency vet info clearly at the top of an info packet that we supply in both digital and hard copies.

While it's important to pick a good emergency vet at a practice that feels safe and practices excellent medicine, we also make sure to have the physically closest emergency hospital number on hand, too. Sometimes our preferred emergency vet and the closest 24/7 emergency vet aren't the same. I hope it will never happen in your life, but sometimes in an emergency a good outcome might rely on a shorter drive.

We picked our emergency vet because it's where Derek practices, but you can get a feel for good emergency vets near you based on conversations with your regular vet. The most important thing about any vet is that you trust them. Trust is paramount. Every dog owner is going to have a different opinion on what makes them trust their vet. Some build trust based on communication; others want a straight-shooter vet who tells it like it is; still others want a gentle vet, or someone who graduated from a specific school. For a lot of people their preferred vet has to do with budget.

Aside from trust, another useful detail to pay attention to is the state of the hospital or practice itself. If the physical environment of the building hasn't been taken care of, it doesn't automatically mean they're practicing bad medicine there, but it's worth paying attention to. Ditto a hospital that refuses to give you a tour. Also, shopping around is totally normal; after all, you might not like the first vet you meet for whatever reason.

That trust thing really is so, so important, though, because only when you trust the vet can you communicate what you need and want. Your dog is beyond important as part of your family, so they deserve to have a doctor who treats them as the precious family member they are.

Pet Insurance

All this talk about veterinarians, emergencies, and specialists probably has you thinking about money, because medicine in America is expensive. I'm gonna let you in on a big secret: Owning pets costs money. Period. There's no way around it—taking good care of your pooch is going to affect your wallet. Making sure they have their vaccinations, they're neutered, they're microchipped, they have regular exams—all of those things are going to cost money and that's okay. It means they're getting the preventative care they need to make them a healthier pet, and also to, you hope, avoid *more* expensive complications down the road as they get older.

Of course, the nature of owning a dog is that at some point in their life they're probably going to require thousands of dollars' worth of care all at once. They're going to get hit by a car or eat something they shouldn't or get diabetes or arthritis or some other nonpreventable disease.

Some people have a savings account where they put money aside every single paycheck like clockwork, just in case. Some people apply for a medical credit card to help pay for big costs. Some people buy pet insurance. Depending on the situation, some humans do all of the above. We've seen and been the people who spend a lot of money on their pets, because pets are family.

One of the things you can do to make the cost of owning a dog easier is invest in pet insurance. Pet insurance can help cover the unforeseen costs associated with both regular and emergency care, as well as things like surgery. Pet insurance isn't so much about saving money as it is about distributing the cost of veterinary care over the lifetime of the pet, whether that be a dog, a cat, a snake, a spider,[84] whatever. If you don't invest in the cost of insurance up front, you'll end up spending money on the other side. Trust me, the dollars get spent either way. Ultimately, pet insurance could be the difference that means having to make a horrible decision between expensive care or—and I shudder to even say the word—euthanasia, simply because of budget.

Some of the big-name, most recommended pet insurance companies include Trupanion, Healthy Paws, Embrace, and Pets Best. Sometimes you can get a break on monthly pet insurance fees by applying for the insurance through your bank or a company you already carry another type of insurance with, like home insurance or car insurance. Saving money is always a good thing.

---

84   I actually don't know if you can insure a spider. I've never tried.

Some of the big national veterinary companies offer their own versions of wellness plans, which offer preventative veterinary care that covers the basics for a monthly or annual cost. Wellness plans tend to cover specific, planned medical issues, like annual vaccinations. If a practice has one of those plans in place, it probably means they've thought a lot about it—but it's always worth it to do your due diligence. Contracts will specify exactly which services they cover and what they'll pay back and when plans kick in after you subscribe to them, so taking the time to read the fine print will make sure you've really covered your tails.

Vaccinations

Vaccinations (or vaccines) are one of the main reasons you and your dog will visit the vet annually for the majority of their life. They're also superimportant at the beginning of your dog's life if you adopt a puppy. Vaccinations start for puppies as early as possible, usually around eight weeks. In all of my dogs' opinions, the best thing about vaccinations is they can almost always be used advantageously in exchange for treats. Yes, there's a little pinch, usually between their shoulder blades, on their back thigh, or somewhere on their front leg, but it really only feels like a bugbite and, like I said: treats. So they make a sad face, flop their big ears down, and wait for the delicious noms to be delivered straight to their mouth. Worth it.

The goal of vaccinations is to protect these little balls of cuteness from a number of dangerous diseases that could potentially be life-threatening . . . but are rendered generally preventable through vaccines. Talk to your vet about which vaccines are important in your region, because some of the details vary from place to place. But no matter where you live, a rabies vaccination and what's called a DAPP vaccine are absolutely recommended for any dog of any lifestyle, from sheepherding working dogs to lazy, sleepy lapdogs who spend most of their time chasing lizards in the backyard, like my pack.

The DAPP vaccine protects against four dangerous diseases, which are actually part of the name. "DAPP" stands for "Distemper, Adenovirus, Parvovirus, and Parainfluenza virus." DAPP. Those four diseases are some of the most common to affect canines, and they're also all highly contagious between dogs.

Canine distemper, sometimes just called *distemper*, is caused by a virus that infects dogs via air or in droplets, usually by other infected animals coughing or sneezing. Distemper affects the body systems dogs use to breathe as well as their GI and central nervous systems. Symptoms vary from dog to dog but include diarrhea, vomiting, and a yellow discharge from the eyes and nose. The few dogs who do survive the disease often live the rest of their lives with seizures and uncontrollable muscular twitches. It's not ideal. Luckily, the vaccine is supereffective. Puppies get the first DAPP shots at eight weeks and then boosters to make sure it's strong in their bodies at twelve and then sixteen weeks old. Adult dogs also get boosters; the vet helps figure out the timing on those.

The "A" in "DAPP" stands for *adenovirus*, which causes infectious canine hepatitis in dogs, affecting their liver, kidneys, eyes, brain, and even their body's ability to clot when injured. Adenovirus is transmitted by animal-to-animal contact; in saliva, feces, and urine; or by contact with inanimate objects that might carry the infection on them, like clothes or furniture.

Dogs who are infected with adenovirus might have symptoms like fever, vomiting, diarrhea, jaundice that causes a yellowing of the skin, and coughing, but as with the other diseases, every dog might look different. Some dogs get "blue eye," where their corneas look cloudy. In puppies, this infection can kill. There's not a specific treatment for canine hepatitis, which is part of why the DAPP vaccine is so darn important. I can't stress that enough.

The first "P" in "DAPP" stands for *parvovirus*, which is frequently shortened down to just "parvo." Parvo is one of the scariest dog diseases, in my opinion. Parvo can affect dogs at any age, but puppies younger than sixteen weeks are the most at risk. Canine parvovirus is shed in the poop of infected animals. The worst thing about parvo is that it's hella contagious *and* it can stay in the environment for months at a time. That's why the vet says no unvaccinated puppies should be out in public before they've had all their shots *and* their boosters. Period. I know there is an intense desire to bring your puppy out to share them with the world, but if a puppy comes into contact with parvovirus, even if the virus has been hanging around for months and months, they can get a life-threatening illness. Parvo causes issues in the GI tract but can also affect the heart; infected dogs usually have bloody diarrhea, vomiting, poor appetite, low energy, and rapid weight loss. Even with aggressive treatment, hospitalization, and quarantine, many dogs die as a result of parvo infection. It's just not worth the risk, especially because the DAPP vaccine is so effective at keeping them protected. Honestly, sometimes I have bad dreams at night about parvo. No thank you, the pack and I opt out.

The last "P" in "DAPP" stands for *parainfluenza*. Canine parainfluenza causes upper airway disease (as in, everything above the lungs) in dogs, which leads to coughing, sneezing, and gunk in their eyes and nose. It's spread by contact with infected snot and mucus. Parainfluenza isn't always quite as serious as something like parvo, but it can inhibit the immune system and make it so that a secondary infection sets in, like pneumonia.

No dogs deserve to suffer from any of these diseases. Given the existence of effective vaccines, it should be a moot point to even worry about your dog dying because of preventable illnesses. I know nobody likes needles, but the idea of being hospitalized with, dying from, or having to be euthanized because of one of these awful diseases sounds way worse.[85] And look, I haven't gotten into the details about rabies, but they're grim. Rabies is a disease that animals carry in their saliva, but humans can be infected by rabies if they're bitten or scratched by an infected animal. Rabies affects the brain and spinal cord. In dogs, rabies can cause foaming at the mouth, seizures, or even paralysis. It's 100 percent fatal, but it's also 100 percent preventable with vaccination. One hundred percent! You can't argue with those numbers, and that's why we suck it up and give our dogs the shot.

Yeah, it hurts. Most of you have had shots before, so you know. Yes, sometimes there are side effects, but the risk of vaccine reaction is minute compared to the risk and severity of the diseases the vaccines prevent. Getting a shot might make your pup sleepy, and the spot where the injection goes might be sore for a little bit. Overall, reactions to vaccines are **overwhelmingly** minor and treatable.

What does a vaccine reaction look like, aside from those minor effects? Good question! Moderate reactions might include vomiting, hives, or facial swelling. I knew a dog once whose ears swelled up after she got her shots, but her humans took her back to the vet and she got a quick dose of steroid and

---

85   All of which will involve being poked with at least one needle, anyways!

antihistamine that cleared it right up. She looked silly with her floppy ears all swollen, but hey—still better than parvo.

Severe vaccine reactions are very rare, but any individual pet can have an individualized reaction. Vomiting, collapse, breathing difficulty, and blue gums would all constitute a serious reaction, and if they happened after leaving the vet you'd turn right around and head back ASAP for help. The severity of a reaction usually correlates to how soon it develops after the vaccine is administered. Even the occasional serious reactions are almost all treatable if promptly addressed. Vaccinations that lead to instant death happen so rarely that they are once-in-a-lifetime experiences for a tiny minority of vets. Even dogs with a history of minor or moderate vaccine reactions can still safely be vaccinated with adjustments, like pretreatment of an antihistamine or staying at the hospital to be monitored for a few hours, just to be safe. As always, talk to your vet if you have concerns. The rule is that if you notice anything you're concerned about—anything, even if you worry it might be minor—you should at minimum call the vet and describe it. Always better to be safe than sorry.

Usually after your pup gets their vaccines or boosters, there's no long-term effects, but every once in a while something funky happens, like a lump under the skin that doesn't go away after more than a week. A lump is another good reason to reach back out to the vet and see what their advice is.

The best part of getting vaccines is having a tag your dog gets to wear on their collar. It's like adding diamonds to a ring, or upgrading the stone in your engagement ring after ten years. Your pooch gets their name tag, their license tag, and their vaccine tag. The tags make a fun tinkling noise when your pup runs around the house, and each tag proves that you love your dog so much you're willing to commit the time and energy and money[86] to protecting them from the scary things that can happen out in the great big world. Just make sure you hold their paw the whole time and tuck them in to baby them after they get their vaccines.

Microchips

I would bet money there are probably videos out on the wild, wild internet talking about microchips and pet tracking as some kind of negative,[87] but microchips are absolutely necessary for pets. No ifs, ands, or thermometers up your butt. It's one of the most reliable ways to identify your dog if they get lost.

The microchip in question is teeny-tiny, about the size of a large grain of rice. Your vet just uses a needle, the same way they give vaccinations.[88] Usually, the chip goes into the same spot, too, in that ruff of extra fur and skin between the shoulder blades. It might sound scary, but pets of all kinds can tolerate it while they're awake. Anyways, most of the time the vet doesn't implant the microchip while your pup is awake; they put it in while the dog is under anesthesia (and sound asleep!) to be neutered. (I haven't talked about that yet, but it's coming; I swear.)

Also, the weirdest (and, in my opinion, the coolest) part is that while the microchip is placed up between your dog's shoulder blades, sometimes, through the course of their lifetime, it *moves*! Your pup can't feel it moving inside them (it's way too small for that), but if they have X-rays done you can

---

86 There are absolutely low-cost vaccination opportunities to be found; pets are expensive, but there are still ways to save money.

87 The Man might be tracking your dog! Tinfoil hats abound.

88 The needle for administering a vaccination is going to be smaller than the one that implants the microchip. Don't stress.

see it on the images. It appears as just a mini speck of white. I've heard stories about it moving all the way down to near a dog's back end, or even shifting from the shoulder down an arm, so the vet has to make sure they scan all over and don't miss it. How weird and awesome is that?

Every microchip is connected to a unique identification number. It's a great backup, in case the dog slips out of or loses their collar. Most vet offices and shelters have a scanner they use to read the microchips. It looks like something from a sci-fi show, but they just hold it over your dog's skin and the info pops up on a digital screen. They can't even feel it. I promise.

Once the microchip is implanted, you'll be able to connect the chip to info about where you live and how to get in touch with you in case your pup gets lost, Dog forbid. Usually, there's a company used to associate your personal info with the microchip. Every year, you pay the company a minuscule annual fee to keep the microchip active. Sometimes there are extra benefits to paying that membership fee (like if your dog gets lost the website will send out a SOS call to other members in the area or help design flyers that can be printed out). Also, paying annually serves as a good time to check the microchip's info to make sure it's up-to-date. When we moved from California to Florida, we had to change every single microchip to make sure the right address was reflected back to us.

It's totally worth it. Don't believe everything the internet tells you about microchips, implanting them, and The Man.

Licenses

After you register your pup with their microchip, you'll also need to pay for your dog's license. No, this will not require a learner's permit and hoping your dog can reach the brake pedal. This license is different from the kind required to operate a motor vehicle.

Okay, yes, licensing is still a government function. In fact, the exact details of licensing your pets vary by county, and it's not limited to dogs, either. Cats usually need licenses, and like I said, depending on where you live, other pets might also need licenses. Many counties have a limit on how many pets one family can keep, so licensing your pets helps your local government keep track of them and makes sure nobody has more pets than they can safely care for.

Usually when undergoing the annual updating of their microchips you also buy their license. Typically, the cost for having a pet licensed isn't very much, unless your pet hasn't been spayed or neutered. That's just a good trick for trying to keep the number of reproducing pets to a minimum. There are already way too many dogs without homes; the world really doesn't need more. (I know, I keep talking about neutering; I promise I'm going to explain it next.)

Also, in order to have a license issued, you usually have to prove you've had your dog vaccinated for rabies. So, you'll submit paperwork that shows vaccination proof and the county issues a license—which is just a piece of paperwork, often one that remains digital, unless you keep paper records—and a rabies tag, which goes on your dog's collar and proves that they're licensed and vaccinated.

In a lot of ways, the license is like a backup to a microchip, associating your dog with you and making sure it's on record that they're part of your family. Just like with microchips, it's also a safety mechanism to help get your dog home in case they're lost or stolen. Let's say your pup sneaks out the back gate, but they have their tag on their collar *and* they're microchipped. If someone finds them, they can bring them to the animal shelter or a local vet, who can scan them for a microchip and look at their tag. Both of those things make sure they get back home.

Last but not least, the license serves as legal documentation in case your dog ever gets into a tussle with another pet while out on a walk or at a dog park. I know, your dog is indubitably very well behaved, but like I said before: not every dog has good manners. In that instance with Roland, reaching out to the other dog's owner would have been useful to get help paying for the cost of medical care and making sure Roland hadn't been exposed to any contagious illnesses. Having an unregistered or unlicensed pet can muddy the waters when it comes to liability and legal ramifications.

I know, it seems like a lot of bureaucracy and paperwork, but that's okay. Your dog is worth the time and effort. I'm the kind of person who keeps digital files and paper backups, so I've got a whole file folder full of information that I keep updated through each pet's life. It means that I love them and I'm doing my very best to care for them in the ways they deserve.

Spaying and Neutering

We have finally arrived at the spaying and neutering section, after all this lead-up. (Round of paw-plause!) Humans are absolutely obsessed with our dogs' junk; it just is what it is. So let's get into it.

Big picture, neutering your dog is important if you aren't going to intentionally breed them. In my opinion, the world already has way too many dogs without homes in it. In the United States alone, there are millions of dogs in shelters.[89] In

---

89   "Pet Statistics," ASPCA, https://www.aspca.org/helping-people-pets /shelter-intake-and-surrender/pet-statistics.

a lifetime, a dog can have up to ten litters. That's at least one dog per litter, if you're talking about the smallest litter possible. (So one unneutered dog makes ten more dogs, but usually they make even more than that.) There are too many pups and not enough places for them, so the most responsible thing you can do is control your dog's ability to reproduce by using surgery as birth control.[90]

A lot of places that adopt out animals as pets require that the pets undergo said surgery before they get to come home. Fair game, in my opinion. Like I said, the overpopulation of unwanted animals in the world is so incomprehensibly huge that you can barely begin to imagine the numbers, so surgicate away!

Lucky for dogs, the risks with these surgeries (either spaying or neutering) are pretty low. The surgery is invasive, it's definitely painful, and it requires pain medication and a two-week recovery period, but none of those things are the worst thing in the world. (I say this as someone who has undergone a total hysterectomy and thus been through a very similar procedure. It's been years now and I can barely remember the hurt anymore. The meds are good. I promise.)

First let's talk about language. Technically, the word "neuter" applies to the surgical removal of an animal's reproductive organ, either in full or in part. "Neuter" applies to animals of either male or female sex, though a lot of people say that dogs with testicles are neutered or castrated and dogs with ovaries are spayed. Sometimes it's also called getting fixed,

---

90   Also, there is a myth that dogs who are genetically related can't sexually reproduce. Biologically related dogs can absolutely get each other pregnant. Sharing genes does not create some kind of birth control.

as in, "Rupert's gonna get fixed soon." An animal who hasn't been neutered is sometimes described as "intact," as in, "Rupert hasn't been fixed yet, so technically he's still intact." Got all that? I don't know why we make things so complicated. I'm just along for the ride.

For male dogs, this surgery involves the removal of their testicles. The vet uses surgical techniques to make an incision in or just in front of their scrotum to take their testicles out. The vet makes sure that important blood vessels inside are carefully tied off so the dog doesn't bleed internally and then the incision is closed using stitches that heal up over about two weeks. In puppies, you probably won't even be able to see the scar. Sometimes, though, if the procedure is performed on an older animal whose testicles have grown to full-size already, a little flap of empty scrotal skin is left behind, kinda like a rudder on a boat. It doesn't hurt anybody—it just looks funny. Very large dogs might have the whole scrotum removed to avoid complications like that excess empty skin rubbing or catching and tearing.

Some dogs might have a retained testicle up in their groin or abdomen, a medical issue called cryptorchidism. It doesn't happen very often, but sometimes when it does it requires multiple incisions instead of just one, or even a more complicated surgery. Cryptorchidism is a highly heritable condition, which means it's typically passed on genetically. Plus, that retained testicle has an increased risk of cancer. Two good reasons for making sure you neuter cryptorchid dogs.

Most male dogs go through puberty before having the surgery performed. Going through puberty is a protective measure for joint and bone health. (If the dog is adopted from an animal shelter, they may be neutered before puberty, just because the humans there are working really hard to handle population control. The effort to reduce overpopulation trumps the benefit to bone and joint health from puberty.) Your vet will be able to advise you on the right timing for your dog, but most dogs become skeletally mature at around a year old. That means (roughly!) that your dog's body is done growing and they can handle going through a surgery like castration. Like I said, that's different for every dog; sometimes the procedure is performed a little bit earlier on small-breed dogs, or a teensy bit later for large- and giant-breed dogs. Great Danes, for example, are usually neutered when they're about a year and a half old. Your dog's vet is the one who knows all the important details, so ask them.

There's not a lot of preventative medical reasons to castrate male dogs besides population control and cryptorchidism, because they don't typically get breast cancer, and testicular or prostate cancers that might develop are usually cured by castration. That might not be true for every dog, though, so don't take my word for it. I haven't been to medical school. Even Derek can't tell you what's right for your dog without knowing all the details.

Sometimes male dogs' behaviors might be affected by being neutered. People say that the surgery sometimes stops them from doing things like territorial urine marking; mounting other pets, people, or furniture;[91] or being aggressive. I've even heard people say some dogs become more cuddly after neutering, but I'm not sure that's true, and there's no good science to prove it. There's also a rumor it makes dogs calmer, but there's no guarantee. Neutering isn't a reliable method for affecting future behavior, especially if a dog is castrated at an older age.

---

91 Rupert has a favorite pillow for this, even post-neuter.

None of my pack right now are female, even though sometimes people call Bashi a girl because of his flowing locks of blond fur,[92] but there is some research that shows spaying female dogs before their first heat can greatly reduce their risk of breast cancer.[93] Wait, before I explain the surgery part, let me explain what "going into heat" means for female dogs.

Going into heat or having a heat cycle is also known as estrus, and it happens for the first time when a female dog reaches puberty at around six to nine months of age. Each heat cycle has stages; a dog who's in the estrus stage is capable of becoming pregnant. Most dogs come into heat about twice a year, roughly every six months, but as with so many things, that number varies by breed and individual. (Younger dogs often have more irregular cycles.)

On average, a dog will be in heat for about a week and a half or two weeks. Their vulva might swell, they will have a fairly substantial amount of bloody vaginal discharge that usually means they have to wear diapers around the house, and they might pee more frequently because their urine has hormones and pheromones in it announcing their reproductive state to other dogs, enticing them to try to mate with them. Dogs in heat are also usually restless and participate in nesting behaviors, often destructively.

Male dogs are superinterested in female dogs who are in heat. Their animal brains want them to do the dirty, what can I say? Females in estrus can become pregnant by any intact

---

92   And because gender is a social construct that dogs don't care about, nor is it linked consistently to external genitalia or other markers of biological sex.

93   "Spay and Neuter Your Pets!," Canine Behavior Program, https://www.brown.edu/Research/Colwill_Lab/CBP/spaynueter.htm.

male, no matter how young, how old, how big, or how small. Heck, sperm can survive for up to a week in the reproductive tract, so a female dog can get pregnant basically anytime during her heat.[94] Pregnancy lasts for about nine weeks, and then there's the whole litter of puppies thing to deal with, so let's go back to the best way to prevent a female dog from getting pregnant in the first place: spaying her.

For females, the surgery is slightly more complicated compared to males. It's officially called an ovo-hysterectomy or an ovariohysterectomy. The vet will make an incision into her abdomen to remove the ovaries and uterus. Sometimes only the ovaries are removed, which is called an oophorectomy or ovariectomy. Again, your vet will recommend which type of spay will be best for your dog, but it remains the most effective form of birth control we have. There are some rare associated potential complications, like an infection of the remaining uterine stump later in life (also known as stump pyometra). Also, even if a spay is performed properly by the vet, ovarian tissue remnants may remain in the abdomen and continue to produce hormones and cause symptoms similar to estrus, which could require a second surgery. Obviously, I can't say this enough, but the humans have **got** to talk to their vet to get the answers to all these questions. Your experience is going to be different from mine with my pack and so on and so forth forever and ever.

In female dogs, estrus is associated with puberty, and going through a first heat can be protective against joint and bone disorders like torn ACLs later in life. The calculation on when to spay comes down to the recommendation of your vet. Look, I told you I couldn't recommend talking to them more. They're the be-all, end-all for good information.

---

94   She can also be impregnated by multiple males.

Like I said earlier, these surgeries require pain meds and a couple of weeks to recover, even though it's a same-day surgery, regardless of sex. Usually, your dog won't get to eat or drink the night before or the morning of the surgery because they're going to go under anesthesia, which is medication that makes them go unconscious so they're not aware of what's going on while surgery is happening. Food or liquid in their stomach means they might regurgitate and choke during surgery, which is clearly something everybody wants to avoid.[95]

The most important part of recovery, besides the cuddles and regularly taking their meds, is that your dog **must** wear their e-collar the whole time they're healing. I know, they're going to look silly and it feels funny and they might walk into corners, but the e-collar will keep them from licking at their stitches or pulling them out and causing infection or trauma that could lead to additional surgery or a visit to the emergency vet. We call it the Cone of Healing at our house, both because if they don't wear it they don't heal, as well as to try to avoid the stigma that comes along with associating it with shame. Healing is good! We like healing!

I cannot emphasize this enough, but do not take off your dog's cone and leave them unsupervised while they're recovering from surgery. If you do take the cone off so they can eat or drink water, you need to be watching them at all times. The cone needs to be immediately replaced after they finish eating or drinking. Leave the cone on. Leave the cone on for the whole time your vet has told you to leave the cone on. Leave the cone on because dogs don't always know what's good for them and if you take it off they absolutely *will* mess with the

---

95   Remember when we talked about aspiration pneumonia and water? Same concept.

incision, at minimum irritating the wound and at worst completely opening it up in a way that requires more surgery to fix. Leave. The. Cone. On.

Often your dog's stitches will dissolve on their own and don't have to be removed by the vet, but there's usually a follow-up appointment just to make sure everything healed up okay. Also, your dog might get a tattoo when they're neutered! How metal is that? Usually, the ink goes on their belly or their ear, just to prove they survived surgery to live another day (without making more pups). The tattoo also helps avoid accidental surgery; once a surgeon sees the tattoo, they'll know they don't need to go in and perform a surgery that's already been done.[96]

Much like vaccination, neutering your dog is one of the most important things you can do for them in their entire life, for a number of reasons. Please make it happen and know that I'm not a hypocrite—I have never had a dog (or cat!) who hasn't been neutered, and I never will.

Random Facts about Dog Anatomy

Derek and I tend to run into the same questions asked over and over again, so here are a few not-so-random facts about dog anatomy that you might not know but probably should because now you have a four-legged friend glued to your hip until they die.

---

96 Feral cats who are released back out to the wild after being neutered will sometimes have the tip of their ear amputated to indicate that they don't need to be trapped and surgicated again. This is a dog book, but a missing ear tip might give a tattooed dog a run for their money in terms of sheer coolness.

First, genetically male dogs also have nipples. They do not use these nipples for nursing in the way that genetic females do after reproduction, but they still have nipples. (Also, you may notice that a female dog who has nursed a litter has enlarged nipples during the nursing process and even permanently after. This is normal.) Your dog's nipples are not growths. They aren't fleas. They don't change anything about your dog's gender. They cannot be removed. There are between eight and ten of them; sometimes more, sometimes fewer. They are a normal part of a dog's anatomy.

Since you are a responsible owner who will have your dog neutered, you don't have to worry about the ins and outs of dog sex. However, sometimes a dog's penis will become visible. Colloquially, this is sometimes called a red rocket or lipstick.

If you've ever seen a red rocket, you'll know immediately why it's called such. It's bright red because it's very vascular. It's also very sensitive. Normally, a dog's entire penis is sheathed into its external foreskin, which is called the prepuce. When a dog is ready to mate, generally aroused, or even kinda excited about something,[97] their penis (also called the glans) will slip out of the prepuce and become exposed. Neutered dogs can also get red rocket. Usually, you can ignore it and it'll go away. Much like eating poop, this is a normal—but, y'know, not ideal—dog behavior.

If a male dog is around an intact female dog in heat, he'll try to mount her. A dog's penis has a bone in it,[98] and near the midpoint of the bone is the bulbus glandis. The bulbus

---

97   Like Rupert with his favorite pillow. Sigh.

98   Unlike the human penis! This bone is called the os penis or baculum. Other animals have a baculum, too, including bats, bears, raccoons, rabbits, nonhuman primates . . . the list goes on and on.

glandis swells up during copulation. The purpose of this anatomical structure is to keep the penis inside the female so that the sperm has an opportunity to get to the egg and implant it, leading to pregnancy. It's not actually a gland at all, because it doesn't secrete anything. After the bulbus glandis swells, the pair of dogs will be stuck together for a short period of time until the swelling goes down. This is often called tying a female, and the bulbus glandis is sometimes called the knot. (Who names this stuff?) That glandular swelling is often mistaken for testicles, but nope.

Occasionally, you may see a yellowish or green discharge at the tip of the penis. This is called smegma, and people sometimes mistake it for pus. Nope! It's a normal lubricant that doesn't need to be wiped away. (Of course, if you see a lot of discharge and your dog is licking himself excessively visit your vet.)

Normally, red rocket just ain't a big deal. You wait for it to go away and that's about all. Sometimes, though, the penis can get stuck outside the sheath and cause a medical situation called paraphimosis. Paraphimosis usually resolves within a few minutes. However, if exposed to air and rough surfaces for too long, the skin of the glans can become dry and irritated. After long enough, it can even swell and take on a purple color. After it swells, it may be difficult for the penis to return to its normal position within the prepuce. Left alone, untreated paraphimosis can lead to infection and even necrosis of the mucous membrane of the glans. Paraphimosis can be caused by many different variables, among them hair or other obstruction wrapped around the base of the penis. If the paraphimosis doesn't go away after four hours, or if the dog is licking excessively or the glans seems particularly irritated, you should see your vet.

Also, since I've brought it up: humping isn't a male-specific dog behavior. All dogs will sometimes hump pillows, toys, or each other. Often humping other dogs (or cats or humans) is a dominance display, but just like humans, dogs also enjoy the sensations that come along with the movement. Training can help.

Postsurgical Considerations

If a veterinarian prescribes an e-collar for your dog, leave the ding-dang, frick-frackin' cone on until you have a follow-up appointment wherein your veterinarian inspects your dog's incision or wound and specifically says that you are permitted to remove the e-collar.

I am friends with brilliant humans. Truly, I know a number of particularly smart humans who excel in a variety of fields. Still, these stupendously intelligent humans decide—without medical degrees—that they should remove their dog's collars so their dog can "have a break." They take off the collar and let the dog roam. The dog continues, unsupervised, and absolutely goes teeth first into licking and biting and nibbling at their incision or wound or *whatever it is the veterinarian is trying to let heal.* Healing wounds are itchy. Healing wounds hurt. Dogs who lick at their wounds aren't cleaning them. They're causing trauma by sanding wounds with their abrasive, rough tongue over and over. (Not to mention the bacteria and germs in their mouth that then enter the wound.) Dogs don't understand why they're wearing an e-collar, but you do. It is your primary, A+, number one responsibility to leave that sucker on until you are specifically ordered to do otherwise. This is so important I made an entire separate second section for it. LEAVE THE CONE ON.

Flea, Tick, and Heartworm Prevention

Almost last but not least, let's talk about fleas (and ticks and heartworms). First, I'm busting the myth that shows up most often: cleanliness doesn't have anything to do with fleas. Our dogs groom themselves daily *and* get dragged to the groomer *and* sometimes the cats groom them, but they're still permanently on flea, tick, and heartworm preventative. It doesn't mean they're dirty and it doesn't mean you're being insulted as an owner. Even the tiniest, cleanest, cutest, purse-living Chihuahua can get fleas. The vast majority of pets with fleas look "clean." You often won't even actually see the fleas because they only live on dogs for a short period of time . . . but just cuz you didn't or can't see 'em doesn't mean they don't exist.

Fleas like to hop onto dogs because they're furry and warm and their blood is delicious. Fleas lay eggs that hatch on dogs, but those eggs can also fall off onto the carpet or furniture. Fleas can lay up to fifty eggs a day. (Ugh, my skin is crawling just thinking about it.) Also, those little suckers are faster than the blink of an eye, and they compress themselves down like a spring so they can jump two hundred times their own body length.[99] Barf. They also carry serious diseases that can be passed along to humans like typhus and the plague. Dogs can even get tapeworm by eating fleas that carry tapeworm larvae. Nobody wins.

Believe it or not, fleas are the number one cause of all itching in dogs, as well as being the number one cause of ear

---

99 "Questions and Answers about Fleas," Community IPM Education Series, May 2007 https://www.canr.msu.edu/ipm/uploads/files /Fleas.pdf.

infection *and* skin infection.[100] Those little suckers are extremely uncomfortable. All our adopted street dogs were covered in fleas when we found them, especially Bashi and Rupert. Just like most other dogs, ours are allergic to flea saliva. It makes their skin inflamed and red. You could literally see the fleas jumping off Bashi during that first bath. It makes me wanna hurl, seriously. Fleas also make dogs' skin smelly and greasy. Also, dogs who are infested with fleas often have a thinner, less luxurious coat. Fleas cause rashes, too.

The itching caused by fleas can also lead to a condition called a hot spot or acute moist dermatitis. Hot spots aren't caused solely by fleas, those little jerks. Anything that causes itching can lead to hot spots, but fleas remain high on the list. Hot spots are basically localized areas of skin inflammation and bacterial infection. Once they set in, your dog then goes after themselves where they're itchy, causing a kind of self-perpetuated "road rash" on their own skin by aggressively licking or chewing to make the itching sensation stop.[101] The hot spot will quickly get worse and spread, creating an oozing, painful lesion that's even worse than what you started with. If your dog has hot spots, it's time to see a vet.[102] Your vet may prescribe antibiotics, anti-inflammatories, or other solutions for treating the underlying cause of the itch, like flea preventative. Also, your dog may have to wear an e-collar while their skin heals.

---

100   "Dermatology Fact Sheets," UC Davis Veterinary Medicine, https://www.vetmed.ucdavis.edu/hospital/animal-health-topics/dermatology-fact-sheets.

101   As someone who has had many surgeries, I can totally comprehend this. The itch that comes from healing wounds can drive you absolutely batty.

102   Are you saying it with me in chorus yet?

Fleas really like warm, humid conditions best, but they exist everywhere in the United States. In every single state, no exaggeration. As a result, every single breed of dog can get fleas. There is no such thing as a flea-resistant pet. The only way to make sure you don't get fleas is to have your dog on flea preventative.

The nice thing about flea preventative is that it's often bundled up with heartworm prevention. Heartworms are a parasitic roundworm spread through mosquito bites. They can be regional, too, so it's important to check with your vet, like with most things. Just to ramp up the ick factor here, adult heartworms like to settle in the blood vessels of the lungs, soaking up all the nutrients from the blood that's pumped from the heart. In advanced infestation, the worms can climb into the right side of the heart, too. They can cause serious infection and lead to death because of congestive heart failure, but they can also cause inflammation and lead to strokes. They *definitely* shorten a dog's life-span. The number one symptom of heartworms is a cough.

The treatment for heartworm infestation sucks, too; my parents' dog Jet, the Pit Bull, had to go through it. He was adopted from the shelter with a heartworm infestation. You treat heartworms with an arsenic-based compound—not even kidding. It's a painful, uncomfortable, risky treatment with the strong possibility of the dog throwing a clot or having a horrible systemic reaction, and every single part of that can be prevented by using a heartworm and flea preventative in the first place. If you live in a place where heartworms are a problem, your dog needs to be tested for them at their annual exam. As a bonus, heartworm preventative meds can also address GI parasites (in most cases).

You should assume you need flea and heartworm prevention unless the vet specifically tells you it isn't useful. The meds aren't complicated, and they don't sting like vaccines do. We give our pack their flea and heartworm meds monthly, though I know there are brands out there you administer every three months instead. The pack likes to chow down on the oral version, which tastes like a treat. There are topical and injectable options, too, but like with a lot of things, you have to talk to the vet about what's going to be right for your pup. The biggest thing to know is that anything that calls itself a flea preventative that you can buy over the counter without a prescription can't be trusted because they're ineffective and sometimes dangerous.[103] The fleas have become resistant to those meds. Unless you get it from a vet, don't expect it to work. (And no, vets aren't trying to scam you out of money when they tell you these meds are important. Do you know how much it costs for a vet to learn how to be a doctor? Most of them will be paying off student loans for their whole lives.)

The last bug I have to talk about is the tick. They're a bit more regionally specific, but they're still an issue for most dogs nationwide. Ticks are a parasitic mite that likes to hitch a ride on people and pets and drink their blood, like fleas do. Their bite also hurts. They bite on and lodge into skin. Ticks can also carry a myriad of nasty diseases that can be passed along to humans, like Lyme disease or Rocky Mountain spotted fever, which is why it's important to be aware of them if you live in an area where they're a problem.

I guess maybe we should be impressed that so many differ-

---

103   CAPSTAR is a fast-acting flea killer that you can get over the counter, but it only lasts twenty-four hours. Think "I'm gonna destroy these suckers from orbit!," not "I'm preventing fleas from showing up at all."

ent little bugs want to take bites out of both us and our dogs, but having been there and done that, I mostly want to avoid ever being on the receiving end of a fleabite again. I'm happy to make sure my pups take their meds regularly, and I know you will be, too. It's better than your pup being some little nasty bugger's dinner!

Dewormer

Just like dealing with fleas, ticks, and heartworms, deworming is an important part of managing parasites in your dog. Dogs, as we have already determined, are pretty gross animals. Thus, it's important to know that almost all dogs become infested with worms at some point in their life.

Roundworms are the most common of the parasitic worms found in dogs, but they can also become infected with hookworm or tapeworm. Puppies can inherit intestinal worms from their mothers; in fact, puppies are frequently infested with worms even in "clean" environments. (Puppies in particular are very susceptible to worms. They pick them up from other adult dogs, or their constant desire to investigate the world around them, or even grooming or swallowing fleas carrying the infective stage of tapeworms. Pretty much every puppy you see is cute as hell and full of worms.)

A puppy infested with worms will have appetite loss, diarrhea, vomiting, and a dull coat. They might drag or scoot their butt across the ground to deal with the itchy feeling of the worms. Parasites steal nutrients, which can stunt growth. They can also induce other illnesses. When heavily infected, puppies may even appear potbellied. Disturbingly, you may be able to see the worms moving around in their poop; tapeworms look like rice grains while roundworms and hookworms look more like spaghetti noodles.[104] Sometimes the worms can travel from the intestines into the puppies' lungs, which, unsurprisingly, causes coughing.[105]

Unfortunately, roundworms also pose a significant risk to humans. Contact with contaminated dog poop can lead to human infection. Roundworm eggs can even accumulate in the soil where pets potty, also leading to human contact and eventual infestation. These infestations can cause eye, lung, heart, and neurological symptoms in people, though there are available treatments. More rarely, humans who accidentally swallow infected fleas can get tapeworm infestations as well. Really, it's best to avoid human infestation entirely by handling dog infestation as soon as possible.

As a result, it's important that puppies are dewormed every two weeks until they're twelve weeks old. After that, up until they're six months old, the schedule shifts to monthly. After six months of age, they can transfer to an adult worming schedule. Most vets recommend monthly deworming because the dewormer is combined in their heartworm treatment, which needs to be administered monthly. (Giving heartworm meds more than roughly forty-five days apart risks the heartworms growing into a stage where they are immune to the dewormer.)

Fecal exams should be conducted two to four times during the first year of your puppy's life and one or two times annually for adults. A negative fecal test doesn't necessarily rule out infestation, as worms and other parasites aren't continuously shed in dogs' poop.

---

104   Sorry if I just put you off your lunch.

105   This entire section, of course, has caused barfing. In you. In me. All of us. Gag.

Your vet can help you pick the dewormer that's right for you and your pet. Normally, there's a do-it-all dewormer that covers all intestinal worms and tapeworms. Like I mentioned earlier, many heartworm preventatives also control for round-worms and other zoonotic GI parasites. Aside from administering dewormer on a monthly schedule, keeping your puppy's living area clean and tidy is useful in preventing and noticing worm infestations.[106]

---

106   Plus, it'll make you feel good, too.

CHAPTER 7

Speaking Dog

If I've said it once, I've said it a million times: every dog has their own behavior and quirks that come with being an individual. Your dog is going to be a teeny-tiny weirdo with a bizarre personality borne from the strangeness of being a dog who has been molded by living with and loving humans. Aside from taking care of them, knowing how to communicate with them is going to be imperative to having a mutually beneficial relationship.

While there is new and exciting research that seems to show dogs understanding English,[107] it's on us to make sure we take the time to know what they're telling us in dog, as it were. The language of dogs is communicated through vocalization, facial expressions, body movement, and even their attitudes toward us. The more time you spend around them, the more fluent you'll become. You'll start to pick up on the nuances of your specific pet, as well as the differences between one dog and another. Here, in broad strokes, are the basics of communicating with your dog in their own vernacular.

---

107 "Research," TheyCanTalk.org, https://www.theycantalk.org/about
/our-approach-to-research. (Those of us who own dogs and speak to
them the way we talk to humans could tell you without a doubt that
they speak our language [English or otherwise].)

Rules for Humans

First and foremost, it's necessary that humans understand a few details about how to interact with dogs from the get-go. Perhaps the most important tool you'll have in your arsenal is the concept of the consent test, which is an idea borrowed from veterinary medicine that, generally speaking, would probably make existing in any society a lot easier if it were better understood.

The concept of consent is often presented to humans through the lens of intimate sexual contact, but the idea of consenting to interaction of all sorts is, generally speaking, not all that complicated. (Nor is it an idea that should be limited to the bedroom.) Consent is agreement or permission to participate in a behavior through affirmative, voluntary actions (or words). Consent requires both communication and respect. Consent is necessary to build strong relationships with any living being, and especially with your dog.

In veterinary medicine, the consent test is practiced by performing a touch or physically advancing into the dog's space and then retreating before evaluating to see if the dog seeks out further interaction. Of course, you don't have to be a doctor in order to perform a consent test with your dog. In fact, though we may frequently practice the concept of consent with dogs by asking their owners if we have permission to say hello or pet their dog, it's less often that we ask the dog's consent to participate.

As an owner (or someone who's about to interact with a dog), you can perform a consent test, too. It's a great way to ask a dog what they want out of their interaction with you. If the dog doesn't belong to you, you should always ask the human for permission first, before initiating any kind of interaction with their dog. It may be that their dog has anxiety, has a history of trauma, just had surgery, or simply isn't good with strangers. By asking a dog's human if you're allowed to say hello, you are potentially avoiding scaring a dog or even being on the receiving end of a possible bite.

It's important to remember that because dogs are individuals, they're going to have differing levels of interest in alone time versus people time; they're even going to have varying preferences when it comes to who they like (and some dogs really only like one human!). Dogs have an incredibly active inner life, just like people do. That just means you might meet a dog who doesn't want to say hi to you on your timeline. Similarly, dogs who are small enough to be picked up might not actually enjoy it. Some dogs are amenable to handling, and even enjoy being kissed or hugged. You can't really train a dog out of their personal preferences here; you just have to respect them and pay attention to their communication.

Also, I'd like to think it goes without saying, but it's good to remind people that you must never, ever interact with a service animal while they're working. Trained service animals have a job to do, and your interruption could possibly put the person who relies on that dog's skills at risk of serious, life-altering injury. You can absolutely watch a service dog do their job, but it would be better for you to just go about your day and act like the dog is simply a normal part of your surroundings. (No disabled people like to be stared at while trying to simply exist in public; I speak from experience here.)

So, let's say the owner of a dog who isn't hard at work gives you the go-ahead to say hi to their pooch. A few rules: Don't come from above or bend down over the top of their heads.

That makes you seem like a big, scary predator, and nobody wants to say hi to someone who terrifies them. Also, don't move too fast. You're new in their world, and moving too fast makes your newness even more overwhelming.

Crouching down to their level is a great signal that you're interested in interaction. Don't put yourself immediately near a dog when you do this; in fact, it's good to keep some distance, avoid direct eye contact, and keep your hands to yourself. You can even turn your body to the side a little to make it clear that you're not dangerous. Don't use treats to try to lure the dog closer; snacks may bring them nearer, but the desire for a snack doesn't actually indicate *I want to physically interact.*

Once you're down where they are, observe their body language in response to your invitation. If the dog increases their distance from you, don't chase them. If they recoil; become submissive, anxious, or fearful (I'll talk specifics about what that looks like later in this chapter); or approach but seem stiff, that dog has communicated they're not actually interested in saying hello. Don't ever force it, even with your own dog. If you do, you're just asking for trouble. At that point, you need to stand up, step back, thank the owner, and go about your day. Remember: It's not personal. We all have off days when we don't want to hang out and chitchat with randos. The same goes for dogs. Also, you don't know that dog's history. They may have had traumatic experiences in their past that make it so saying hi to someone new really is a fight-or-flight moment. Stepping away and respecting their boundaries may help teach them it's safe to interact next time, too.

Once you bend down and make it clear you want to interact, the dog may come closer to indicate they're interested in saying hi. You can simply offer a hand to them, palm up, and allow them to sniff, nudge, or nuzzle your palm. The palm-up approach is especially useful for a tentative dog, but it's not a bad idea to give any dog the ability to check out your smell and what you're all about in such a nonthreatening manner.

Depending on their response to your hand, you may be able to pat their chest, neck, or flank once or twice before seeing if they let you know they're into it and want more. If they pass the consent test by jumping on you, saying hi, nudging you, leaning into or onto you, or having loose and wiggly body language, you're probably good to go. If they withdraw or don't seem psyched about you, you need to pay attention to their signals and move on. Only interact with dogs to the degree that they're clearly enthusiastic about. As with so many other areas in life, unless you get an enthusiastic yes, it's an absolute no. Behave accordingly.

Tails

Dogs' tails tell us a lot about how they're currently feeling in their body. Of course, not every dog is a Labrador with a deadly weapon attached to their butt.[108] Some dogs have short tails by nature or because their tails have been docked.[109] Despite this, there are a few tail-related behaviors that you can pay attention to—and that even dogs with very short or no tails can still participate in.

---

108   The tail, not their ability to clear the room with a stinky fart.

109   A barbaric practice that, along with ear cropping, shouldn't exist, because it is physical mutilation with no basis in science: Joe Dunne, "Why Crop a Dog's Ears?" VetHelpDirect, February 24, 2021, https://vethelpdirect.com/vetblog/2021/02/24/why-crop-a-dogs-ears/.

Perhaps the most familiar to people is tail wagging. A dog wagging their tail is generally perceived as an expression of happiness, but it's important to note that tail wagging is simply an expression of stimulation. In fact, some aggressive dogs wag their tail as part of their warning display before participating in escalation behavior.

The counterpoint to a wagging tail is a tucked tail. Some dogs will tuck their tail all the way between their back legs so you almost can't see it at all. A tucked tail is an expression of the dog being scared, anxious, and/or nervous. A dog who is tucking their tail is trying to make themselves appear smaller because they're experiencing negative emotion.

A tail that's straight up also can express stimulation, but it most frequently means a dog is paying close attention. You can see this body language often displayed in hunting dogs who are on the trail, or even in dogs who hear a noise that interests them.

However, as with spoken or signed language, there's almost always multiple things you have to notice in order to understand the whole message that's being conveyed. A tail will tell you part of the story, but it's important to pay attention to the whole dog.

Ears

Much like tails, dogs have a wide variety of different ear shapes and sizes. Their ears are controlled by eighteen muscles that allow them to raise, lower, rotate, tilt, and move them independently for better hearing and emotional expression. (Cats have thirty-two. Humans have six, but I can't even wiggle my ears.)

Ears that are up and facing forward usually mean that the dog is paying attention, and often that they're listening closely. (Ears and tail all up is a typical combination.) Moving ears in general typically indicate that the dog is paying attention to the sounds going on around them. Sometimes they'll even move their ear specifically to better hear a noise in the direction it's coming from.

Ears that are pinned back are like a tucked tail. This is an expression of fear, and sometimes a precursor to aggressive behavior. Pinned ears mean you should be paying close attention to what's going on with the dog you're interacting with.

Relaxed ears are going to vary from dog to dog. A blond Papillon mix named Bashi with fluffy floppy ears is going to have a different chill face than, say, a maniac of a Rat Terrier named Rupert with giant triangular sailboat ears that are always at attention. Generally speaking, though, when relaxed, a dog's ears are in their natural position. They won't be putting effort or muscle movement into positioning them.

Ears are excellent indicators as to where and how a dog is paying attention, but just like with tails, they only tell a part of the story. The next thing to focus on is your dog's eyes.

Eyes

I cannot count all the hours I have spent lovingly gazing into my dogs' eyes. It constitutes a vast chunk of my life, and I don't regret one second of it. However, it's actually kinda weird my dogs don't mind me looking directly in their eyes. They've learned that I'm not trying to dominate them but that I'm communicating that I love them with my entire heart. Looking directly at a dog is context dependent. The more direct you're being with your gaze, the more you risk confrontation or the possibility of communicating that you're interested in a confrontation. The more indirect your eyeline and body language, the less threatening you come across to a dog.

Your dogs might not be comfortable with this and *that's okay*. Again, my dogs aren't going to be the same as your dogs and that's a beautiful thing. Variety is the spice of life, baby.

Normally you're going to see a little bit of the whites of a dog's eyes, mostly on the top and bottom. As they use their peepers to peer around, you might notice that some dogs have more visible white than others. The whites of their eyes are most visible when they're looking at you, but their body is oriented away from you, or if they're checking you out from one side.

The big thing to notice about those whites is when you can really see them. This is colloquially called whale eye, and it usually means a dog is frightened or feels threatened. It's often the precursor to a fear bite or warning bite, sometimes even without a growl. (I'll chat about sounds soon!)

Whale eye happens when your dog's eyes widen to make the sclera more visible. Whale eye is often accompanied by a closed mouth, a tense face, and upright or pinned-back ears. Whale eye doesn't always mean your dog is about to be aggressive—Ezra has really bad teeth, and he's had to have multiple mouth surgeries. If he's in pain, he'll run to his bed and give me whale eye to let me know he's tapping out. I always try to give him space at this moment because he's done a very clear and good job of letting me know he's reached his limit. Lucky for me, he always lets me love on him again (eventually).

Dogs also have what's called a third eyelid, or nictitating membrane.[110] This is a thin, opaque tissue that rests in the inner corner of the eye, below the lower eyelid. It helps protect the eye and cornea, and it spreads tears across the eyeball's surface, keeping it nice and moist.

Normally, you won't see your dog's third eyelid. Occasionally, you might catch a glance when they're superrelaxed and falling asleep. This can also happen when they're medicated or coming out of sedation or anesthesia. Generally, though, the third eyelid is only visible as an indicator of illness or a painful eye. This third eyelid can also prolapse, typically after a tear gland has become inflamed. In this case, it looks like a red, swollen mass on the lower eyelid near the nose or muzzle. This prolapse is usually called cherry eye because of the color. Cherry eye means a trip to the vet for surgical or nonsurgical treatment, depending on the dog. Cherry eye can be uncomfortable, and it certainly looks painful—but it's not an indicator of the dog's emotional experience or part of what they're trying to communicate to you.[111]

---

110 One hundred percent a great band name, along with tapetum lucidum, a layer of tissue in the eye of many vertebrates (including dogs) that reflects visible light back through the retina, improving their night vision and causing a visible eyeshine, especially in photographs. Maybe *Tapetum Lucidum* is Nictitating Membrane's debut album. They would obviously be a death metal band that solely covers songs with dog-related lyrics.

111 Unless you count the third eyelid as a communication along the lines of, *Ow, please take me to fix this.*

Mouth

Dogs' mouths do a lot of work in the communication depart-ment. Obviously, they don't have the same ability to create language in the way that we do—but they say plenty to us all the same. Many humans make the mistake of trying to train their dogs out of using their mouths to communicate, incor-rectly assuming that training the dog to stop will serve as a deterrent for what the human perceives to be negative behav-ior. Unfortunately, what they often end up doing is training the dog to stop giving context clues for escalation of negativity or aggression. This will frequently lead to a dog who's been trained not to growl—and so instead of growling before moving up the next step in their communication (snapping or biting), they immediately go straight to biting without warning. This doesn't serve anyone. Mouths are important to pay attention to, and instead of training a dog to *not* growl, it's our job to fig-ure out what's causing the dog to behave in such a manner and adjust appropriately.

A growl is also sometimes called a snarl. It can be a very frightening noise—intentionally so, even from a little dog. They're trying to let you know they mean business. They are uncomfortable and unhappy with something in their environ-ment. A growl is a warning sign and often (but not always) a precursor to a bite. If you get bitten after a dog growls at you, it is often because you, the human, have created an unreason-able situation by missing their communication cues or vio-lating their clear boundaries. It is almost always the human's fault they got bitten. This is why speaking dog is integral. Even the smallest Chihuahua is still descended from a wolf.

Sometimes an uplifted lip comes along with a growl. This is a clear signal of a dog's intent to use their teeth. This also comes before a bite—but you don't always get a lot of time between the uplifted lip and the bite. An uplifted lip means: *Back the frick up. You are violating a boundary of mine, and if you continue, I will be forced to escalate.* Much like the growl, this must be paid attention to but should not be trained out of your dog.

Less scary than growling or lifted lips is the stress yawn. A stress yawn is different from a regular yawn, and context clues matter in this situation. As far as we can tell, a stress yawn is part of self-soothing when a dog feels anxious or uneasy. You might see your dog stress yawning when hearing you fight with your partner, or if a stranger approaches and your dog is not feeling up for interaction. You can tell that the yawn indicates stress based on the rest of their body language: it might be accompanied by a tucked tail, pinned ears, whale eye, or avoiding eye contact.

Dog yawns that aren't related to stress come along with a number of theories, including the idea that they might play a role in stimulating the nervous system or cooling down the brain during temperature increases. As always, take in the full-body picture when assessing your dog's yawn.

Like a yawn, panting can be an indication that a dog is feeling a level of anxiety, fear, or stress. Bashi pants a lot when there are fireworks going off in the neighborhood; he's terrified by them, and his body is letting me know how scared he feels. Anxiety panting usually means you need to figure out what's stressing your pup out and, if possible, remove them from the situation. As I discussed before, dogs don't sweat the way people do, so they also pant when they need to cool down. Say it with me, class: pay attention to the whole dog to understand what they're saying, not just one part of them!

Finally, one of the things many new dog owners notice

is that their dog might lick their lips repeatedly. If there's no food around, lip licking is typically a gesture of discomfort. Typically, dogs will lick their lips when they feel threatened by something around them. The goal of lip licking is to ward off perceived aggression. You might see lip licking in combination with averted eyes—for example, if you scold your dog for having a potty accident indoors hours after the accident has happened and they don't connect your frustration with something they did previously. They may, however, now perceive you as a threat because you are upset and potentially angry. They're trying to tell you that they're not a threat when they see you as behaving aggressively.

Lip licking may also happen when dogs are feeling frustrated or confused. If you notice your dog licking their lips at the end of a long training session, especially if they're not catching on to what you're trying to teach them, they may be signaling to you that their brains are done training for the day.

Finally, lip licking may be indicative of your dog being in pain—but I'll talk about that in more detail at the end of this chapter.

Sounds

Dogs use those cute little mouths of theirs to do more than make faces. They're also very good at making noises (or vocalizing, if you wanna get fancy with it). Some dogs go their whole lives without making much noise; Roland was a very quiet dog, and when he barked it sounded like someone was strangling a rubber chicken.[112] Rupert is the exact opposite. I don't think

---

112   This might have been why he was so quiet all the time. He didn't want the other dogs to make fun of him.

I've ever met such a chatty dog. Every dog is going to have their own voice, but we have a general idea of what groups of sounds mean, even if the specifics are individualized. Sounds, like all other communication, require context. Make sure you look at your dog as a whole before trying to interpret what they're talking to you about.

First off is the bark. There are as many different barks as there are dog breeds. In fact, there's probably more. Barks differ from breed to breed and even from dog to dog. Some breeds are more prone to barking than others. Sometimes the way one breed talks is different from how another breed does. Shiba Inus are renowned for having a very specific way of conversing with their owners. Huskies are big on full-throated serenades. Papillons bark at every single thing that might possibly move. Beagles like to make sure the whole neighborhood can hear them.

Make sure you do some research before you bring a dog home so you know what you're getting into. If you live in a tiny apartment and don't want a high-energy, loud dog, you need to make sure you're picking one who has the right communication style to fit in with your life.

Howls are a bit like barking, if you took a bark and pulled it like taffy to make it long. Some dogs are more likely to howl than others. Some dogs howl for the sheer joy of it. Some dogs howl to communicate with their pack. Occasionally, a howl may specifically communicate anxiety or distress. Howling can be very, very cute.

On the other hand, a whine or a cry (or prolonged crying) can be one of the most distressing things to hear when you're a dog owner. Whining isn't always an indicator that your dog is suffering. It can also mean they want something (like, say, that treat up on the countertop out of their reach). A whine can also be an expression of concern; Bashi will sometimes whine if I'm upset. A whine can also mean they're stressed—Derek deals with a lot of whining and crying in the emergency room, especially when dogs are undergoing procedures and their family isn't nearby. A cry doesn't have to be a bad thing, but it can absolutely tug at the heartstrings. A cry also doesn't necessarily mean a dog is hurt; I'll discuss that in greater detail soon.

Finally, you might notice that your dog is . . . well, that your dog is sneezing at you. It's not a real sneeze, per se, like the kind where you have springtime allergies. It's a bit like when a toddler or small child pretend sneezes. A sneeze is usually used by a dog to get you to pay attention to them. It's a little bit like saying, "Hey!" It can also be a noise they make when they're in a good mood and playing around. I feel particularly special when old man Henry sneezes at me because it means he's having a lovely day and he wants me to join in.

Body Language

All of the facial expressions I've just discussed are part of a dog's body language; the vocabulary of their communication, so to speak. The rest of their body contributes to the sentence structure of their communication, too! It can be a lot to think about all these concepts when they're new, but you'll pick up on what your dog is putting down quicker than you expect, especially if you're doing the work of paying close attention. They spend their whole day using their entire body to communicate. It's an easy language to immerse yourself in.

One of the most familiar images when it comes to canines is "raised hackles." Hackles are the hairs that stand up along your dog's neck and back in a reflexive triggering of the sympathetic nervous system (which causes the fight-or-flight response). The act of the hairs physically standing up is called piloerection; it's something humans experience, too—sometimes when we're scared, or even if we hear a song that emotionally moves us. (Birds and cats have hackles, too. You've likely seen the image of a black cat around Halloween, tail standing straight up and their fur fully raised.)

Dogs have special muscles called the arrector pili muscles that contract around the hair follicle to make the hairs stand up. This causes the dog to appear larger and taller, which serves as a visual warning to threats (other animals, people, whatever) that a dog is ready to leap into action. Raised hackles don't necessarily mean aggression, but they do mean a willingness to participate in confrontation. It's the dog's version of, "Come at me, bro." It means the dog is on high alert, but unconsciously. Raised hackles can be caused by fear, surprise, or unease, too.

Some breeds of dog have more prominent hackles (Rhodesian Ridgebacks look like their hackles are always raised), while others are harder to differentiate (like poodles). Raised hackles can even happen during playtime; it's just a matter of making sure your dog doesn't graduate from an unconscious body reaction to an assertive aggression, especially when interacting with other people or animals.

Like raised hackles, many people have a mental image of dogs "pointing" when they picture them. A dog "points" by freezing their body stock still, pointing their nose at a particular spot, and usually lifting one front paw—like they're pointing it at something.

Not all dogs point. It's somewhat instinctive in some breeds (especially retrievers, spaniels, and setters), but it's otherwise mostly a learned behavior. In dogs who have been historically bred to hunt, it may be a reaction to seeing what their brain considers prey. It's a way of telling you to look where they're paying attention—which is kind of a cool collaboration, if you think about it. It may also be part of planning their pounce or trying to stalk in anticipation of an ambush. If your dog isn't a natural pointer, they can be taught—but this isn't the right book for that, as you already know. Go find a trainer!

Another mental image that comes along with picturing dogs in general is that of the play bow. The play bow involves a dog bending down on the elbows of their front paws, ears perky or forward, head down, tail up, and butt wagging away. Often their mouth will be open, tongue lolling. This is an expression of excitement, and an open invitation to play! Sometimes dogs get so excited when play bowing that they'll even bark—but they won't usually growl. A play bow means: *Pay attention to me! I have energy and I want to spend time with you!* Play bows can be directed at other dogs, people, or even other animals. Rupert loves to play bow at the cats before they get all tangled up and wild. I try to always respond to a play bow, even if only for a few minutes. After all, our dogs aren't around forever. It's when they're gone that you think about the missed opportunities you could have spent indulging with them.

Some people may notice that their dogs are doing a lot of paw licking, which they then misinterpret as a sign of being nervous. Overwhelmingly, paw licking has to do with being itchy, and I'm gonna send you back up to the health chapter (chapter 6) to reread the subsection about flea, tick, and heartworm prevention.

A dog who rolls over to show their belly may also be communicating to you that they're inviting play (or at least belly rubs, in Bashi's case), but rolling on their side or back can also be a sign of submission. Submission can be a sign of respect and trust, or it can be a sign of fearfulness. As always, you need to pay attention to the whole body to get the full story. Submissive bellies may come along with other signs of submission, like lowering their gaze away from yours, or licking another dog's chin. Submissive bellies can sometimes come with submissive urination, where a dog uncontrollably pees as a result of their anxiety or fear. This can happen especially in dogs with traumatic backgrounds of abuse. Submission can be a normal dog behavior, but overly submissive dogs may need to work with a trainer to build confidence and become more comfortable.

Finally, it's important to point out that the act of lifting a leg to pee or squatting to pee is not associated with one sex or the other. Many dogs with penises squat to urinate; many dogs without lift their legs to pee. As I noted before, gender roles don't matter when you're a dog. How they pee is going to have everything to do with what feels comfortable in their body and nothing to do with our idea of masculinity or femininity. Don't get too wrapped up with how your dog chooses to urinate.

Types of Aggression

Sometimes people end up with aggressive dogs they don't know how to handle, don't know how to deal with, and don't know how to talk about. It can be extremely isolating to have an aggressive dog. People may end up in a situation they never could have imagined, dealing with a dog who's well out of their ability to control, with no idea how to get help.

I hope this book will help with that. Getting a dog is obviously a big responsibility, and making sure you're doing it right from start to finish will help minimize the likelihood of an uncontrollable, aggressive dog. Understanding how to communicate with and to your dog will also help. I cannot over-state the importance of training; even a beginner training class is worth the investment of time, energy, and money. However, you can do everything right and still end up with an aggressive dog—either your own dog or one you're interacting with. Being able to understand the type of aggression they're displaying will help you make the best decisions moving forward.

Veterinary medicine has a specialty called veterinary be-haviorism that focuses specifically on how pets behave and what we can do as their family to help adjust behaviors so that they lead happy, healthy lives. If you're dealing with a dog who has behavioral issues, veterinary behaviorists are some of the most highly educated specialists out there and they'll be able to guide you along to figure things out.

Veterinary medicine has some specific ways to describe aggression that may help with understanding the kind of be-havior and attitude you're dealing with when interacting with an aggressive dog. These behaviors may be short-lived, or they may be chronic. It's going to be entirely situational and, as al-ways, dependent upon a variety of variables (including the in-dividual dog).

Fear aggression tends to show up as a reluctance to interact—a dog who gives you all the signals before they be-come physically aggressive, from showcasing pinned ears to raised hackles to a snarl and a tucked tail. Fear aggression is usually demonstrated in some kind of sign of retreat before a bite or attack. It might be as simple as a bit of whale eye or it might show up as a full-on cower, but there will be clear behavioral signs. Dogs dealing with fear aggression usually try to increase the distance between themselves and whatever or whoever they feel is threatening them. They want to get the heck away, and fast. Their bodies are often obliquely oriented away from the threat as they try with all their might to communicate that they are not interested in a confrontation.

Confident aggression may sound like a misnomer, but it's contrasted with fear aggression in that this dog typically wants to close the distance between themselves and the threat instead of increasing the distance by retreating. A dog expressing this kind of confident aggression will square up, eyes focused on you, tail up. In some cases, they might even be confused for a happy dog, especially if you're not familiar with the signs of dog communication.[113] Their aggression is not necessarily about being territorial, though it's often thought of as such.

Territorial aggression, however, is specifically focused on an area. This aggression doesn't have to happen only at home, either. In some cases, a dog expressing territorial aggression may do so in places like a veterinary exam room they're only in for a few minutes. This kind of aggression often has to do with the dog's perspective of who got there first. It may even be minimized by the veterinarian entering the exam room first or already being present when the dog comes in. Territorial aggression has to do with location, but the behavior may manifest as confident or fearful aggression depending on the dog.

One of the most important things you can do to protect yourself and the people around you if you own an aggressive dog is first seek out specialists to guide you. There are options, including medication, behavioral training, and even physical devices to help, like a muzzle. If you have an aggressive dog you have to bring out in public for something like a veterinary exam, it's important to let your veterinarian know beforehand

---

113   Derek says that in some dogs it's literally because they're happy to
      attack you. Whatever makes you feel good, I guess.

so they can advise you as to how to safely approach the situation. This also allows your veterinary staff to protect themselves and the other people and pets who might be coming for appointments.

If you're out in public and you run into an aggressive dog on a leash, pay attention to what their behavior is telegraphing and give them ample space. Obviously, this isn't the kind of dog you want to stop and try to interact with. If you run into an aggressive dog who does not appear to have humans around, please call your local animal control services for assistance and advice.

In very rare situations, after all other solutions have been exhausted, behavioral euthanasia may be considered for an aggressive dog. Many veterinarians are uncomfortable talking about death at all, and the discussion of behavioral euthanasia is a difficult and nuanced one that is only considered as a very last option. It is, however, an option—especially if people, including children, and other pets are at risk because of the aggressive dog's behavior.

Please reach out to your veterinarian for help if you end up in a situation like this. In our in-home euthanasia practice, Derek and I have only dealt with two situations that required behavioral euthanasia. Coming to the decision was extremely difficult for the family and only done after years of other attempted intervention. We have also had to make the difficult decision to euthanize our own adopted dog after she bit both of us multiple times, once severely dislocating my wrist. It is one of the hardest things we've ever had to do, after many attempts at other types of intervention, and we would not wish the experience on anyone else. Dealing with an aggressive dog can be physically and emotionally exhausting and overwhelming, but you don't have to deal with it alone.

How Dogs Show Pain

As a final note, it's important that we talk about how dogs express pain. Humans have a tendency to interpret an animal's behavior through the lens of our own experiences. It's important to recognize that dogs have a complexity of experience that makes them uniquely special, but they aren't humans. That's part of why we love them.

As a result, a lot of times when we see our dogs panting, shivering, shaking, or acting restless, we assume that they're expressing fear or anxiety. After all, that's what we do, right? However, all of those behaviors are much more commonly related to expressions of pain in dogs, not fear. Along with panting, shivering, shaking, and restlessness, dogs also show that they're in pain by limping. Sometimes they'll also severely reduce their normal activity in order to minimize their pain. They're less likely to engage in play or general frivolity, but sometimes they'll still try.

Often they'll have a hard time sleeping when they're in pain. Unlike humans, they're less likely to vocalize when they're in pain. In fact, they may not yelp, yip, pull away, or otherwise "act" as though they're in pain, even when you touch the painful spot.

Dogs are extremely good at masking (or not expressing) when they're in acute or chronic pain. Part of this likely has to do with their roots. An animal in pain is often an animal that can be picked off as prey, so it's imperative to put forth a facade of strength.

You can pay attention to their appetite; many dogs will reduce how much they eat when they're in pain. (Though, as usual, this doesn't apply to every dog. Many have great appetites, even when in substantial pain.) You can also often notice that they may lick or chew at a painful spot, even if there isn't a visible wound. If they lick or chew themselves to the point of causing injury or creating a hot spot, they're probably hurting.

Derek and I meet with many well-meaning owners who fail to recognize when their dog is in obvious pain because they simply don't connect the dots that dogs experience the world differently than we do. We'll often try talking them through the thought experiment: So, your dog is limping? *Yes.* What does it feel like in your body when you limp? *It hurts.* Does limping usually happen because you're uncomfortable? *Yes, it's an expression of being in pain.* Can you keep doing it if you can't get to the doctor for a few days? *Of course, if I have to.* Your dog is relying on you to get them to the doctor, and they're going to tough it out if that doesn't happen.

There are sometimes so many similarities between us and our dogs that it's easy to erase the differences that divide us from our canine companions. However, remembering that your new family member is a wonderful, beautiful, gorgeous dog and therefore experiences the world differently from you is the best way you can ensure that you care for them exactly the way they need.

CHAPTER 8

Resources
and Paperwork

Pet Sitter Guide

Here's the information we give when someone pet sits our dogs. We email them a copy, we make sure our closest contacts have a copy, and we put a hard copy on the fridge. We also make sure to give them a copy of our house key.

Contact Info

This one seems basic but is probably the most important. Make sure this information is clear and easy to read.

> Your Full Name | Your Phone Number
> Your Significant Other's Full Name | Their Phone Number
> Your Local Contact | Their Phone Number
> Your Pet Sitter's Full Name(s) | Their Phone Number(s)
> Your 24-Hour Emergency Vet Name |
> Their Phone Number and Address |
> Written directions from your house to their office
> Your Nonemergency Vet Name |
> Their Phone Number and Address

Schedule

How long will you be gone? Leave dates and times for your departure and return. If multiple people will be pet sitting for you, leave the schedule for when they'll be at and leaving your house.

Pets

Make sure you include your pet's name and their defining characteristics, especially if there are multiple pets in the house.

Example:

> Bashi (blond, barks a lot)
> Rupert (anxious Rat Terrier, more anxious without Ace)
> Ezra (skinny shadow, head shy)
> Henry (ancient black puppy boy)

Meals

Leave all pertinent meal information for your pet sitter. Include how often your dog eats, when your dog normally eats, where the food is located in the house, and how much food needs to be measured out for each dog. We keep a measuring cup that's the appropriate amount of dog food for all pets in our dog food container, so everyone just needs "one scoop."

Example:

> 2x a day, all—they'll usually wake you up around 7:00 am and they start begging for dinner at 5:00 pm. They usually receive a third meal right before a late human bedtime, around midnight or 1:00 am. Refill water dishes at night.

> Henry: 1 scoop
> Everyone else: 2 scoops
> Add some water and a tiny bit of wet food (in fridge)
> All dogs eat in their crates with the door shut, doesn't
> matter which crate they go into

Medications

If any of your dogs are on medications, include the meds, how often they need to be applied, the appropriate dosages, and where the medications are located. If the meds don't have to be refrigerated, we normally put the meds by the dog food on the counter. Don't forget important info like whether or not the meds need to be given with food.

Example:

> Henry:
> 4 drops of ear meds in each ear
> 6-pound dose of meloxicam (1.5mL) in food once daily[114]

Notes

This is where I leave all the other information that doesn't have a place so far, like reminders to take off their collars before they go into their crates, or that they need to be crated if left alone for more than thirty minutes. If your dog absolutely cannot sleep without their favorite purple toy, this is the place for that info.

---

114   Many medications for dogs are dosed according to size. Henry weighs six pounds, so a six-pound dose is equivalent to 1.5mL of medication.

Finally, don't forget to leave your Wi-Fi network and password, plus how your TV turns on and where the remotes are. You'd be surprised at how frequently this gets forgotten. We live in a house that was built out of cinder block in the 1960s, so without Wi-Fi access your phone is basically a brick. Pet sitters gotta know this stuff!

Dog Tags

I talked about it way earlier in the book, but our dogs all have tags on their collars with important information on them. One is a contact tag. The second is a rabies vaccination tag. Bashi is an escape artist, so he has a third tag with a scannable QR code that includes another way to contact us—just in case.

The front of each contact tag has their full name. Our dogs all have ridiculous names and titles, which is why that info usually takes up the entirety of the front of the tag. Like this:

> Bashi
>
> "Red Alert"
>
> The Youngest

The first name is the nickname for Sebastian. His nickname Red Alert is because of his propensity to bark and warn us about every single thing that breathes or moves outside. Finally, at one point he was "The Youngest" in our household of much older geriatric animals. He no longer fits that bill, but the name stuck. This just goes to show you that the sky's the limit with your dog's name. (Mister Ezra Inkspot, Rupert Ripper Winglet, and Henry Amos Abner, if you were wondering about the others.)

On the backs of the tags are our last names. (We use Calhoon-Ratcliff for joint tags since we both retained our last names after we got married.) We also list three phone numbers: mine, Derek's, and a third local contact, just in case we can't be reached in an emergency. In this case, we list mine first because I'm the most likely to pick up the phone. Derek's is second, as the second owner, and my mom is the third, because she's not us, but she's also good about answering the telephone.

The rabies tags are provided to us by our county. Bashi's extra tags exist in the very limited chance that he might somehow sneak out of or lose his other tags. One of the extra tags is provided by the company that is connected to his microchip; the second extra tag was purchased from Dynotag,[115] a smart tag company that allows you to connect any information you want to a scannable QR code. Dynotags can be used for all kinds of stuff, not just dog tags, but the tag works beautifully.

Additional Resources and Websites

For easy access, here are some of the websites I've mentioned in this book. These sites are those we either use regularly in our household or recommend to other pet owners as invaluable resources.

ASPCA: https://www.aspca.org

The American Society for the Prevention of Cruelty to Animals was one of the first humane societies established in North America and is now one of the largest global humane societies. Programs exist to assist with adoption, veterinary care including spay/neuter operations, investigating animal cruelty cases on small and large scales, and even surrendering lost and found pets.

---

115   Dynotag.com.

The Humane Society:

https://www.humanesociety.org

Established in 1954, the Humane Society of the United States provides rescue, response, and sanctuary work while offering hands-on animal care services to end animal cruelty and care for animals in need.

PAWS: https://www.paws.org

Since 1967, PAWS has helped shelter and adopt out homeless cats and dogs and educate the community about compassion and caring for animals while helping wild and domesticated animals thrive in whatever space is best for them.

PetMD: https://www.petmd.com

PetMD has been around for fifteen years. Their mission is focused on collaborating with a network of credible veterinarians in an effort to bring the general public the most up-to-date and accurate pet health information for all things pet health.

Veterinary Partner:

https://www.veterinarypartner.com

Veterinary Partner is an online resource that is, according to the veterinarypartner.com website, "the latest incarnation of" the Veterinary Information Network, Inc., founded more than thirty years ago, and provides "the finest and most accurate pet health information" for client education. Categories are organized by pet type and search terms can be used to narrow down specific articles.

Pet Poison Helpline:

https://www.petpoisonhelpline.com

(855) 764-7661

Pet Poison Helpline is a twenty-four-hour animal poison control service available through the United States, Canada, and the Caribbean for pet owners and veterinary professionals who need assistance with treating a potentially poisoned pet. The Pet Poison Helpline accepts a one-time incident fee of seventy-five dollars to evaluate the poisoning and determine if the pet can be monitored from home or should be taken in to see their vet. If veterinary care is necessary, the Helpline will work together with your veterinarian to develop a specific treatment plan for your pet.

Animal Poison Control Center (APCC):

https://www.aspca.org/pet-care/animal-poison-control

(888) 426-4435

The ASPCA Animal Poison Control Center is a twenty-four-hour-a-day, 365-days-a-year helpline to assist with animal poison-related emergencies. Similar to the Pet Poison Helpline, a consultation fee may apply. The APCC's website also includes a number of valuable resources for pet owners, including information about poisonous plants, foods, and household products.

They Can Talk: https://www.theycantalk.org

"A community-generated site dedicated to helping people teach learners to communicate using sound board Augmentative Interspecies Communication (AIC) Devices. Founded by a cognitive scientist, this site brings together tips and tricks for using specialized buttons and tiles to help communicate with your dog—and let your dog talk back."

CHAPTER 9

So Long, Farewell

Okay, y'all. We've made it this far, and if you haven't learned at least one new thing about your dog I have failed at my job. Honestly, I didn't realize I could write more than a chapter about dogs. I guess I really am an expert, huh? By this point, I really have covered pretty much everything for the basics. I think it's probably fair to say I went a little beyond that, too, but as they say: knowledge is power.

I'm finishing this book the same way I started, sitting in my studio, surrounded by my pack. There's a dog sharing my seat with me and two sprawled out across the dog bed that permanently occupies the corner next to my desk. Every few sentences, I reach over and give someone a pat. We're close to dinnertime and the subsequent two-mile walk, so I have to be careful to not move too much or they can get the wrong idea that I'm finished writing and it's time! to! go! There's honestly nothing I love more than their company.[116]

You and your dog will probably use more than a few tips or tricks from this book. As with any individual relationship, you'll also find yourself adapting in order to meet the needs and expectations of yourself and your pup. Use your veterinarian as the integral resource that they are after all that education they survived. Talk to other dog people in order to learn

---

116 Sorry, Derek. Sorry, rest of my family. I'm pretty sure all y'all already know this, though.

more about what works for you and what doesn't. If you can't find it in these pages, do some research. What we know about dogs seems to expand and grow every year. What I've written here might end up outdated a decade from now.[117] Also, don't trust a person who doesn't like dogs—or whom your dog doesn't like. I swear they have an extrasensory perception that weeds out the worst in humanity.

Don't forget to treat your relationship with your dog as something that can grow and change instead of remaining static. I'm a better dog parent[118] now with Rupert than I was with Roland almost two decades ago. I'm more patient, more kind, and I've got so much more knowledge than I did as a teenager. The dog who inevitably comes after Rupert[119] will benefit from all the lessons I learned with him.[120]

More than anything, I hope that your journey with your new dog will be one that encapsulates a relationship like the one I have with each member of my pack, built on mutual trust, respect, full-fledged adoration, and a hefty dose of love. I am their caretaker, yes, but we're also family. There are a million and one pithy sayings I could quote at you,[121] but I think the most important lesson is that dogs teach us unconditional

---

117   Maybe my publisher will let me release a new edition, eh?

118   I don't love "dog owner." They seem to have too much sentience for this to not feel sus to me. YMMV.

119   "Life is a series of dogs."

120   Ugh. Dog forbid. I hope I'll be heading toward fifty before that happens. Dogs never die, right? RIGHT?!

121   "Be the person your dog thinks you are." "The best therapist has fur and four legs." "The better I get to know men, the more I find myself loving dogs." Throw these suckers on a coffee mug and call it a day, boyos!

love. If you can manage that even once in your lifetime, you've done better than most. Good luck, Dogspeed, and don't forget to send me some pictures of your furball.[122]

---

122   You can find pics of my pack all over social media, but especially on Twitter using #SWBKpets. ("SWBK" stands for "Stay Weird, Be Kind.")

Acknowledgments

Though they will likely never be able to read it, this book is and always will be for my pack. For the dogs who have already been and those who will come to be, thank you for saving my life every single day. You have all truly kept me anchored here. You make me a better human every day. *I love you. Be good dogs.*

All my love to Derek, for recognizing that "love is an action you must repeat ceaselessly." (And to Andrew Davidson, for writing that sentence.)

Every gratitude to Rose and Georgia, for always reading the words I write.

All the thanks to my agent, Stacia Decker, for taking a chance on a rando in her inbox with questions about publishing, and to my editor, Ronnie Alvarado, for letting this book breathe a little. It's all the better for both of you. Michael Anderson, thank you for thinking of me in the first place. You're literally why this book exists. And thank you to Emma Taussig, for keeping us all on track.

Last but never least, my family. Life is a series of dogs, and it wouldn't have been without y'all. Love you and all your beasts.

I'm sure I've forgotten to say thank-you to somebody important. I hope you'll still love me, anyways.

Appendix

Important Veterinary Visits for Your Dog

By now, you might be feeling a little bit overwhelmed about all the information you have to keep in your head about your new dog—but don't stress. Kinda like parenting (which, admittedly, I haven't done. With a human. I'm great with my niblings, though.[123]), you'll figure it out as you go. However, here's an easy appendix for the important veterinary visits you'll need to make through your dog's life.

Eight Weeks: The First Vet Visit

- Physical exam
- Core vaccine, first shot (DAPP)
- Fecal test (to determine GI worm infestation status)

---

123 Gender-neutral term for "nieces and nephews." Technically the gender-neutral term for aunt (or uncle) is "ankle" or "auncle," but "Ankle Ace" sounds too silly even for me.

- Dewormer (administered even if GI worm negative, to eradicate infestation)
- Start flea and heartworm preventative, depending on product and pet weight

Hopefully, per "The First Eight Weeks" section of chapter 6, you haven't adopted a dog under the age of eight weeks so they can continue the very important tasks of socializing and learning how to dog from mom and their other littermates. However the process for the core vaccinations can be administered to puppies as young as six weeks old.

During this visit, your dog will be given a physical exam to check that their body looks good and they're the right body weight. They'll have a fecal exam to test for the presence of hookworms or roundworms (which are zoonotic, as you know). They'll also receive the first dose of their core vaccines (DAPP). They will not receive their rabies vaccination yet; this comes later.

Without giving you a full immunology class lecture, puppies take in maternal antibodies (or immunoglobulins) through their intestines. These antibodies are absorbed over their first few meals of mother's milk, called colostrum.[124] Colostrum is produced for a day or two in the mama dog, and it's packed full of these antibodies as well as other key nutrients. Doctors sometimes call colostrum "liquid gold" due to its ingredients. In their mom's body, these antibodies protect her by providing her immunity to diseases. Once the puppy consumes the colostrum, they circulate around its body as it's growing, provid-

---

124   A protein used by the immune system to neutralize foreign objects in the body like bacteria and viruses. https://vetfocus.royalcanin.com /en/scientific/canine-colostrum.

ing the same immunity. Unfortunately, these antibodies only hang around for six to twelve weeks before being gradually eliminated by your puppy's own immune system. Also, not all puppies get the same amount of colostrum, and therefore they might not all have the same level of antibodies.

There's not a tried-and-true timeline for when these maternal antibodies leave your pup's system, either, so sometimes vaccinations administered at six weeks will be rendered inactive by the maternal antibodies fighting them—the maternal antibodies take one look at the antigen[125] in the vaccination, latch on, and get rid of them, often before your puppy's new immune system can do any work. This is great for protecting your puppy, but not great for building a healthy immune system, which has to become familiar with a virus in order to kick its butt during an infection. This is why we usually do the first round of vaccines at eight weeks. This is also why we don't give the rabies vaccine until further down the line; the maternal antibodies will gobble it up and no immunity will be built.

Ten to Fourteen Weeks

- Physical exam
- Core vaccine booster (DAPP)
- Bordetella vaccine (optional, discuss with your vet)
- Leptospirosis vaccine (optional, discuss with your vet)
- Fecal test
- Dewormer

---

125   Any substance that causes the immune system to produce antibodies against it.

Sixteen Weeks

- Physical exam
- Core vaccine booster (DAPP)
- Rabies vaccine
- Bordetella booster (optional, discuss with your vet)
- Leptospirosis booster (optional, discuss with your vet)
- Fecal test
- Dewormer
- Start flea and heartworm preventative

Each subsequent visit up to sixteen weeks of age will also include a physical exam plus the same fecal test as before. Aside from these, the most important parts of these visits are boosters of the core vaccines. Boosters are basically extra doses of a vaccine, intended to enhance the protection offered by the first vaccine. They can also begin immunization in the case that a previous vaccine was blocked by those maternal antibodies still hanging around. By the time your puppy hits sixteen weeks old, they'll likely have had two to four rounds of vaccinations and boosters, depending on what your veterinarian recommends. You shouldn't go longer than four weeks between boosters; by the time you hit a month out, the efficacy is lost and you have to start from scratch.

Although it's sorely tempting to bring your pup out to show them off and socialize them with the world, their own immune system will not be fully developed until they're sixteen weeks of age and done with all their shots. Without a fully mature immune system, their likelihood of getting sick is significantly increased. Please don't put your pup at risk; wait and let the medicine do its job. Derek has had the soul-crushing and avoidable experience of having to euthanize whole litters of puppies that had been infected with parvo and weren't going to survive, instead of letting them die painful deaths due to the disease. This isn't just a case-study, it's real life. Protect your pup, y'all.

At their sixteen-week appointment, your dog will receive their first rabies vaccine. Unlike the core vaccines or some of the optional vaccines, the rabies vaccine is a single shot.

Please remember that variability will exist in this timeline for each pet, depending on their breed, life experience, and body. Your vet is the most important tool you can rely on through this process. Let them guide you.

One Year

- Physical exam
- One year vaccines (DAPP, rabies, optional vaccines per recommendation)
- Neuter surgery
- Dental exam

Assuming no emergencies, once your dog has completed their puppy vaccines, your veterinarian won't need to see either of you until your dog hits their first birthday. They should be able to provide you with a flea and heartworm prescription that can be refilled without an in-person visit every single time.

Neuter surgery will be appropriate once your dog has reached skeletal maturity. As we talked about earlier, if you rescue your dog from a shelter, they may already have undergone this surgery because the shelter is trying to ensure your dog doesn't go on to make many more dogs. For small breeds, this surgery may happen earlier. For large breed dogs, it might be later. Talk to your vet about the right timeline for you and your family.

Their first birthday is also the right time to start talking to your vet about a full dental performed under anesthesia. Remember that an ounce of prevention is worth a pound of cure.[126]

Two to Seven Years

- Physical exam
- Fecal test
- Complete blood panel
- Urinalysis
- Dental exam

At this point, your dog is a bona fide adult. Again, assuming no emergencies, you should bring them in to see the vet for an annual exam (as in, once every year). This will usually include a physical exam and some bloodwork, which screens for organ health (kidney and liver function) and excludes chronic illnesses. A urinalysis will check their urinary system function, and a fecal exam will make sure no GI parasites have gotten them sick.[127] Depending on the dog, dentals will happen every one to three years.

Dogs age roughly six to ten times faster than humans, which means adhering to a schedule of annual exams is like seeing your doctor once a decade. It's worth it just to make sure everything is hunky-dory, trust me.

---

126   It's easier to stop something from happening in the first place than it is to repair damage after the fact. This absolutely applies to gum disease.

127   But your dog has been on flea and heartworm prevention since they were a puppy, so this shouldn't be an issue. Wink emoji.

Seven Years to Forever

- Physical exam
- Fecal test
- Complete blood panel
- Urinalysis
- Dental exam
- X-rays
- Thyroid screening

Once your dog hits seven years (again, this will vary depending on your dog and your veterinarian's recommendations), their annual exams will now become semiannual, occurring every six months. This exam will likely include X-rays to check for cancer and a thyroid panel to make sure their thyroid is doing everything it's supposed to being doing.

You'll remain on this schedule until it's time to talk to your vet about hospice, palliative care, and/or euthanasia. I'm not going to get into those details here because, being completely honest, that's an entire book unto itself.

I cannot stress enough that your veterinarian is your most powerful ally in the quest to keep your dog healthy, happy, and around for as long as possible. Don't be afraid to ask them questions. Rely on them. Use their knowledge to extend the life of your pet. And pay for the pet insurance, trust me on that one.

Index

Index

Index

Index

Index

About the Author

ACE TILTON RATCLIFF is a multidisciplinary artist and writer who lives and works in sunny South Florida. In 2017, Ace cofounded Harper's Promise with their veterinarian husband, Dr. Derek Calhoon. HP is an in-home veterinary practice focused on end-of-life hospice, palliative, and euthanasia care.

Ace is a sucker for the literal underdog: they live with four dogs and three cats, all abandoned street animals. They're an amateur beekeeper who loves to collect plants. Their free time is spent getting tattooed or riding their scooter to the beach to read. You can find them online @mortuaryreport or at stayweirdbekind.com.